D1165032

changing rooms colour

To Ruby

This book is published to accompany the television series
Changing Rooms which is produced by Bazal (part of
GMG Endemol Entertainment) for BBC TV.

Executive Producer: Linda Clifford
Producers: Ann Hill and Caspar Peacock

Published by BBC Worldwide Ltd,
80 Wood Lane, London W12 0TT

First published 1999

© Linda Barker & Bazal 1999
The moral right of the author has been asserted.

Rooms designed by: Linda Barker, Laurence Llewelyn-Bowen,
Michael Jewitt, Anna Ryder Richardson and Graham Wynne.
DIY Handyman: Andy Kane

All rights reserved. No part of this book may be reproduced in
any form or by any means, without permission in writing from
the publisher, except by a reviewer who may quote brief
passages in a review.

ISBN 0 563 55112 7

Photographs by Ed Reeve © BBC Worldwide Ltd 1999

Text written in conjunction with Helen Chislett
Commissioning Editor: Nicky Copeland
Project Editor: Sally Potter
Art Director/Concept Design: Lisa Pettibone
Cover Design: Lisa Pettibone
Book Design: Kathryn Gammon
Picture Research: Susannah Parker
Stylists: Catherine Huckerby; Marcia Morgan; Mary Norden

Paint on cover photo supplied by: Living Rooms, 172 Leith Walk,
Edinburgh EH6 5EB. For stocklists call 0131 561 1903.
Tins supplied by: Sheibarg Can Manufacturers, Cutler Heights
Lane, Bradford BD4 9HZ, tel 01274 661 757

Set in Rotis Sans Serif
Printed and bound in France by Imprimerie Pollina s.a.
Colour origination by Radstock Reproductions, Midsomer Norton
Jacket printed in France by Imprimerie Pollina s.a.

In describing these projects, every care has been taken to recom-
mend the safest ways of working. The publishers and the author
cannot accept any legal responsibility or liability for accidents or
damage arising from the use of any items mentioned, or in the
carrying out of any of the projects described in this book.

changing rooms colour

Linda Barker

BBC

contents

open your

Anyone who has seen *Changing Rooms* will know that we use a lot of bright colour on the programme. Love it or hate it, colour is the one element that always gets a response. From the moment the lid of the paint can is prised off, the audience is second-guessing whether the owners will cry with happiness or dismay.

Not that the programme seems to have deterred viewers from using colour – far from it. If anything, it has shown that the days of 'safe' hints of colour and oceans of calming magnolia are well and truly behind us. Not everyone wants gutsy red or tangy green in their home, but with so many shades to choose from, it really is possible to find something for everyone.

As I stress over and over again in this book, using colour means finding out what is right for you rather than copying ideas from books or television programmes: these can provide inspiration, but not the finished result. I see myself as an ice queen, and given the chance would live in a cool palace filled with creamy whites, frozen blues and sharp silvers, so in my own home I am drawn towards the neutral palette – a far cry from many of the designs I create on *Changing Rooms*. But that is not to say I dislike intense colours: in fact, I love them and can sometimes feel my heart racing with anticipation as I start to apply a bold colour to a wall. That is the other wonderful thing about using colour: its power to affect our moods – stimulating

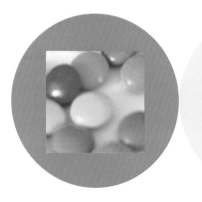  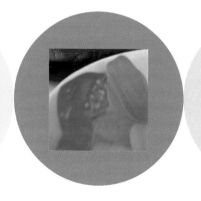 

mind

us into action or simply helping us to wind down.

In this book I have highlighted four families of colour that are wonderful to work with:

- **Bread and butter** – natural colour
- **Sugared almonds** – pastel shades
- **Summer pudding** – vivid colour
- **Wine gums** – deep colour (vibrant colours with the edge knocked off)

It is no coincidence that I have chosen titles based around delicious foods: colour is such a sensual entity that you really can almost taste it, smell it and feel it. Part of the delight of working with it is recognizing just how much it touches nerves deep within us. This is not to say that my four groups are the only choices. As you explore with colour yourself, you will find that there are many routes to follow once you have sufficient confidence.

I haven't used diagrams of colour wheels or scientific analyses of colour combinations in this book. Because these methods are so technical, they often discourage people from experimenting with colour. My approach is more instinctive and hands-on, and the book reflects this. However, it is useful to know some jargon, so there is a glossary of essential colour-speak on page 14.

The rooms I have chosen to illustrate each section of this book were designed by myself and *Changing Rooms* designers Laurence Llewelyn-Bowen, Michael Jewitt, Anna Ryder Richardson and Graham Wynne, and have all been featured on *Changing Rooms* (except for my own living room and bedroom). I hope you will use them as a springboard for your ideas, rather than as a blueprint for your own home.

It is always interesting to see how a room has been put together, but it is just as interesting to come up with your own colour choices. See which colour combinations on these pages strike a chord with you, then read how to use them yourself. There are step-by-step creative effects for you to copy, and plenty of my own decorating secrets for you to share. I hope that by the end of the book you will be brimming with colour confidence, ready to wield the paintbrush like a magic wand around your home.

So swallow your prejudices and open your mind. Colour is such an important part of life that it is well worth mastering. And take it from me – it is so uplifting to create a room that pleases you by doing nothing more than giving it a change of colour. What could be more magical than that?

where to st

My first piece of advice is this: don't be frightened of colour. We live surrounded by it, and the trick is to find the family of colours closest to your heart. Open your eyes to the world around you – a cornfield against a blue sky, a beach in early morning mist, autumn leaves on a path washed with rain ... these are the sort of images that inspire a vivid use of colour.

Personally, I tend not to use colour wheels or sample boards. They have many uses but they can't

take account of the way light moves around your home, the shape of the rooms, or the possessions you already have that must be comfortably integrated. Instead, begin your planning by gathering together items from all over the house that you love for their colour. These might be favourite clothes or scarves, pots or plates, cushions or ribbons, lipsticks or soaps, postcards or paper – anything goes. Open your wardrobe and look at the colours you like wearing – this should give you

the colour basics

a clue as to how brave you would like to be with the walls. Now clear a table and make a sort of still-life arrangement of all these goodies. Don't worry about scale: just add, reject and generally mess around with the assortment until you begin to recognize which colours and combinations you are instinctively drawn towards. These are the ones you should surround yourself with in your home.

Rules and How to Break Them

In many people's minds there are definite rules about colour and they worry about breaking them. You can, in fact, put any colours together as long as they have the same depth of tone (see page 14). Think of the pinks, creams and blues of seashells, or the golds and russets of autumn leaves. Nature understands how to mix all sorts of colours. She combines myriad colours in landscape and individual creatures, yet nothing ever clashes. This is what we need to take our cue from. Learn to recognize what makes a successful combination. If, on the other hand, you are someone who loves to live with the excitement of clashing colours, then that is fine, too – just get cracking and enjoy your boldness and sense of fun.

It is too simplistic to say that certain colours are suitable for certain rooms. Green, for example, is often considered to be ideal in bedrooms because of its restful qualities, yellow for kitchens because it is said to be sunny and welcoming, cream for living rooms so that no one will tire of it, red for studies because it is so stimulating. But there is far more to colour than these ideas suggest. It is the shade you choose, what you combine it with, how much of it you use and how the light hits it that really determine what effect it will have in a room.

The function of a room must be taken into consideration when choosing your colour scheme, but that doesn't mean sacrificing the colours you really want to the notion of being sensible. If you have young children, dogs and a longing for a cream space, don't listen to those who tell you it would be foolish. Admittedly, you will have to think about practicalities – wipe-down satinwood paint, washable covers, hard flooring – but you can still have your cream room and a happy family. Believe me, Ribena does come off light-coloured sofa cushions, but you should probably Scotchguard them anyway.

See the Light

Never ever underestimate the importance of light – natural or artificial – in a room. Light plays all kinds of tricks on colour, not all of them kind, and you must have an understanding of this when choosing your colours.

First think about what time of day the room is likely to be most used. A dining room, for example, might have very poor natural light, but that won't necessarily matter if you are using it mainly for candlelit dinners (see page 45).

Spend a few days really looking at how much light comes into a room and which direction it moves in. Remember, too, that the cold northern light we get in the UK is rarely bright enough to take the shocking pinks and canary yellows found in the Caribbean. The muddier the colour, the better suited it is to our light: think ochre, lavender or sage rather than canary, cobalt or emerald.

Don't forget to consider the effect of artificial lighting in a room, too. Conventional lightbulbs give a warm orange light, whereas fluorescent lighting has a cold blue quality that never brings out the best in a colour. Halogen light is a favourite with designers because it has a clean, clear light which is true to colours (see page 43). Overhead lighting can be flat and uninspiring, which is why many designers don't use it at all. If you do have an overhead light, put it on a dimmer switch so that you can control it. Artificial light looks best when layered, so bring in lots of other light sources – table lamps, wall lights, task lighting (for reading or working), candles and so on. The idea is to bring out the best in your chosen colours by lighting them well at all times of the day.

Colours can be tailored to suit the available light. Blues do not have to appear cold; the addition of magenta will warm them. Yellows, on the other hand, which have a reputation for warmth, can be cooled down to shades of vanilla ice-cream or lemon sorbet. How cool or warm a colour is depends on the amount of magenta it contains.

Shapes and Sizes

Just as light plays tricks on colour, so colour plays tricks on the shape and size of rooms. Cool colours containing more blue than red make the walls of a room appear to recede, while warm colours containing more red than blue seem to bring them in.

However, with so many paint techniques to choose from, even this basic rule has been bent. Applied decoration, such as colour-washing or stencilling, allows you to add another layer to the wall colour, giving the illusion of looking through to the solid colour behind. This means that you *can* use dark, powerful colours in the smallest of rooms, such as bathrooms and hallways, and they won't necessarily make the space appear smaller, as long as you break them up in some way.

There are many other tricks of the trade … You can make a ceiling appear higher by painting it in a light colour (see page 107), or bring it down by continuing the ceiling colour to picture rail height or painting it darker than the walls. Shading the walls darker towards the floor will make the room seem higher as the eye travels upwards. You can make awkward-shaped rooms recede with pale, unifying shades, or make sloping ceilings seem intimate by painting them the same as the walls. You can use vertical stripes to make a room look higher, or horizontal ones to make it look bigger (see page 60). You can hide ugly corners by drawing the eye towards a patch of bright colour elsewhere, or make a wonderful display area by painting one

wall a completely different shade to the rest. Picture or dado rails are useful to divide different finishes: if you don't have the real thing, you can always fake the same effect with a painted stripe. These tricks are all part of the professional decorator's kit-bag, but they are easy to copy in your own home.

Also think about using colour to unify spaces in your home. If you want to make a house appear bigger internally, choose pale colours that are all in sympathy with one another so that there is a feeling of continuity from one room to the next. Conversely, you might want to create a dramatic effect by leading the eye from fiery red to forest green. Part of creating the effect you want means deciding whether you are decorating for your own pleasure or to have an impact on those who come to visit. There is no right or wrong in this decision; it is all a question of personal taste. In design, rules are meant to be broken.

Essential paint

Paint falls into two categories: water-based and oil-based. Use water-based paints if possible because, apart from being kinder to the environment, they are easier to use (you can clean brushes with water) and don't smell so strongly. New paint technology is advancing all the time and water-based products are now as tough as old boots, which means they can match the durability of their oil-based rivals. There's even a water-based metal paint now, for use on metal.

Flat finish or matt finish paints are non-reflective. Eggshell has a low sheen, slightly more lustrous than a flat finish. Semi-gloss, (some satins, silks and eggshells), also has lustre, but is not highly reflective. High gloss paint (used on wood or metal) is the most reflective.

Brush Care

Using water-based paints means that you can clean brushes with warm soapy water. Rub the bristles right up to the heel of the brush with your fingertips, and rinse until the water runs clear. Hang brushes up by the hole in the handle so that water runs away from the metal part and air can circulate easily around the bristles.

After using oil-based paint, clean brushes in white spirit. Squeeze the bristles with a rubber-gloved hand, then rinse again in white spirit.

Rollers

Use synthetic sleeves for water-based paints, and lamb's-wool sleeves for oil-based ones. When painting rough surfaces, use rollers with longer pile. Caution: cheap rollers roll unevenly and smear paint.

Using Paint

On the whole, when talking about colour, we're actually thinking about the walls. They surround us and give us a feeling of being wrapped up in colour. Paint is the most versatile colour medium because it is instant, accessible and comes in thousands and thousands of colour choices. So how do you find the one you want? Well, go back to that still life you made earlier (see page 9) and get your paint sample charts in front of you. Now whittle the selection of still-life items down to a family of colours you really love – perhaps two or three shades – and choose a paint sample to match. Generally speaking, the idea is to find a colour you adore and then take it down a notch or two: this allows for the fact that it will have a lot more impact on four walls than it does on a small swatch. If you plan on being really adventurous, play safe first by buying a small sample pot (250ml) of your chosen colour and applying the entire contents to a piece of cardboard or MDF. Now prop it up against the wall and live with it for at least a week, remembering to move it around to different corners of the room and to study it in all lights. Still love it? Then this is the one for you.

Don't be alarmed when you put your chosen paint on the walls and it doesn't look right. With no flooring, furniture or accessories, any colour can look off-putting. It's also true that a tiny paint sample will never give you a completely accurate indication of what four walls will look like in the same shade. If you think you have overdone it, don't despair – look for a way of making the colour less solid through some sort of paint technique or applied decoration. This might be a freehand mural (see page 69), a horizontal stripe (see page 60), or perhaps a bold stencil (see page 125). A more contemporary twist is to use blocks of colour in a room, perhaps by painting one wall a really startling shade and using more sombre tones on the other three. Remember that you can't really tell whether or not you like a colour until you have added all the other ingredients to a room. It is not unusual on *Changing Rooms* for our neighbours to get cold feet halfway through the first day: huge blocks of colour on their own do look very stark and intimidating. Have the courage of your convictions and keep with it at this stage.

You might also choose to use contrasting colours, which are known as accents. These often

Key Colour Words

Accent colours: Sharp colours chosen to lift a scheme. For example, perhaps you love hot pink, but in a fashion context you might choose to wear a hot pink scarf with a black suit rather than a pink suit with black shoes. That pink scarf is your accent colour.

Base colour: The colour used in the greatest proportions – usually the wall shade. It has often been chosen because it makes the perfect canvas on which to introduce contrasts, accents or colours that complement each other.

Clashing colours: These create an extreme effect – when you want colours to vibrate in front of you and still resonate when you close your eyes. Juxtaposition is all-important when designing a clash, so make sure you go for maximum impact.

Cold colours: These shades contain lots of blue. You can have cool greys, for example, that make you shiver as you put them on the wall, but that doesn't mean all greys are cold. If they contain lots of magenta, they take on quite a different character.

Contrasting colours: These are used when you want to give a room heart-stopping impact – perhaps by placing burnt-orange cushions against a cool blue background.

Contrasting colours never come from the same family.

Dominant colour: This sort of colour stands head and shoulders over others. It is not necessarily the one used in the largest proportions, but the one that has attitude.

Family of colours: This term applies to colours that are in some way related. The blue family, for example, might also include shades of greeny-blue at one end and purples at the other. Browns might stretch from coffee and taupe (brownish-grey) through to pale shades of orange and red.

Highlights: An alternative name for accent colours.

Warm colours: These contain lots of magenta. Even blues can be warm, so don't be deterred from using them because you feel they will look cold.

Toning colours: These are colours of the same tonal value – they share a depth of tone. The idea is that you can successfully combine a strong yellow with a strong blue, for example, but a strong yellow with a soft blue might be disastrous. These colours are not necessarily from the same family, but have the same amount of red or blue in them. If the colours complement each other and none is fighting for attention over the others, the colours are said to be toning.

completely change the character of the wall paint. They allow you to dress a room up or down, to make it more punchy or restful, to add grandeur or humour. Don't be tied to the notion that your ceiling and woodwork must stay brilliant white. Although it was a technological marvel when first invented, brilliant white often does other colours no favours at all. Look instead towards creams and old-fashioned whites which suit our northern light far better.

For the purposes of television, we usually work with paint on walls. This is because £500 is a tight budget and we have rigid time constraints. But, of course, you also have the choice of wallpapers and tiles. Wallpaper has a very different effect – a diffusion of colour that gives it quite a textural feel. Tiles are also available in many wonderful varieties. I often use them as an accent colour in a kitchen or bathroom as their hardness makes them ideal for breaking up large expanses of wall colour (see page 123). Don't forget that they can now be painted any shade you want, so if you have inherited some really horrible tiles, you can either tile on top of them or give them a new lease of life with paint. Use a tile primer, then compatible solvent-based paint and varnish.

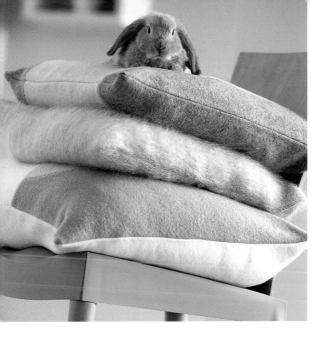

Textural Treats

If there is one big design story of the moment, it is texture and the impact it is making on our homes. Perhaps you have always preferred eggshell to gloss, but now you have to take that notion a step further. Metallics have returned, not necessarily to be used as paint colour, but as glazes that can be layered over other colours to give them a whole new dimension (see page 60). Alternatively, they could be used to jazz up furniture, as with the aluminium leaf appliqué on page 77. These reflective surfaces are beautiful and dramatic, and definitely the Next Big Thing.

But texture is not just about combining matt surfaces with gloss ones; it is also about how the roughness or smoothness of something changes and affects colours, be it on walls, floors, windows or furniture. Fashion designers, such as Jasper Conran, have shown how it is possible to create subtle colour variation through different weaves and finishes. Making over a room no longer means adding just new colour; it also involves looking at how to layer textures to give the room interest and definition (see page 20). Curtains and soft furnishings have all become more important recently; just think what a huge impact suede, velvet, fur and chenille have had on our homes in the last five years. On *Changing Rooms* we have used everything from concrete slabs and driftwood to dustsheets and pebbles to enhance the textural aspect of rooms.

So there you have it – simple really, isn't it? Now join me in a closer look at some of the designs we created on *Changing Rooms* and see how colour has been applied to startling effect.

utter

I am walking on Camber Sands near Rye in Sussex. It is autumn and above me is a crisp blue sky with seagulls wheeling overhead. The sea is grey and so are the pebbles beneath my feet. Yet, if I look more closely, I can see infinite varieties of delicate colour within the stones, from creamy white and honey gold to dove grey and slate black. It is images like these that set me buzzing.

Some might say that naturals are not proper colours, but they are, in fact, as valid as red or blue. Certainly we don't use them a lot on *Changing Rooms*, but that is because they are so subtle that a TV camera rarely does them justice. In my own home I use a lot of soft colours from the naturals palette – winter whites, taupe, putty and stone (see page 24). There is a certain intensity or hue within them that I like very much.

Natural colours conjure up savoury images of

farmhouse cheeses, wholemeal bread, oatmeal biscuits and the dark shiny surface of fresh mackerel: the simple good things of life. You can also draw abundant inspiration from the natural world, be it from rocks such as limestone, granite or slate, woods such as maple, sycamore or beech, or plants such as barley and wheat. Naturals make me think of Scandinavian interiors with a clean, bleached look; fabrics such as cotton, canvas or linen; or clothes by Donna Karan and Nicole Farhi. The natural palette appeals to both sight and touch: think of the contrast between rough undyed calico and a stone table, or the simplicity of a pale wooden bowl laid on top of a bamboo mat. In fact, in this part of the spectrum texture is almost as important as the colours themselves.

How to Use Naturals

Naturals work best in rooms with good light, and are ideal for our cool northern variety. Muted blends of woods, white and cream make relaxing backdrops for living, the idea being to have colours that work in harmony rather than fight for attention. But you also have the option of introducing flashes of more definite colour now and again – perhaps with a change of tablecloth or seating throw – according to your mood, or the season.

The naturals palette is also a very easy way of decorating. All whites work well together, be they blue-whites, pink-whites, yellow-whites or grey-whites. As they incorporate shades of other colours, they change according to what they are near. The only colour I am not so keen on is brilliant white, which is actually very intrusive. I have found that I am drawn more towards the softer, old-fashioned spectrum of whites, which is better in northern light.

Any space, from modern loft-style apartments through to period homes, looks great in naturals. What counts are the proportions of the room and the light within it – architectural detailing is not important. This is not to say that naturals have no place in smaller houses, but you would struggle to give them as much impact in a tiny cottage with dark beamed ceilings.

The important thing if opting for this palette is to embrace the idea of layering textures and subtle

colours within a room. Natural shades are sometimes not strong enough to work as flat colour – they can look very dull – so they need the other dimension of surface variation. Although they appear to be the most uncontrived and simple of interiors, they demand the most skill to do well – just as the natural look in make-up is one of the hardest to achieve. It is not just a question of choosing a suitable shade for the walls, but in deciding whether it should be applied to a textured surface such as rough plaster or Italian stucco (see page 31). Each ingredient, be it floor, furniture or even flowers, must hold its own in the total scheme, but not overwhelm it. For this reason, an accent colour here is more likely to be chocolate brown or iron grey than acid green or shocking pink. Naturals demand great discipline: no single object should unsettle the total look, and if that means living without favourite things, so be it. Having said that, it can be liberating to scale down belongings to the few that really matter and work well. Naturals don't have to mean minimalism, but they do require purism and simplicity. When they work well, they are breathtakingly beautiful and also very sensual: the tactile dimension means that fingers will delight in them just as much as eyes.

Ingredients

You need never buy conventional carpet again if you opt for the natural approach. Sanded floor-boards that are then varnished, bleached or limed make the perfect foil for natural shades. Parquet flooring is a more sophisticated option, and again makes an ideal base for this range of colours. Or choose natural floor coverings, such as coir, sea-grass, sisal or jute, which not only blend into the mood but also introduce more texture to the room.

Windows can be dressed with simple wooden shutters, billowing calico, delicate lace panels or swathes of soft muslin. The choice you make should reflect the wall surfaces, flooring and general ambience of the room. It will also depend on whether you are trying to frame a perfect view or block out the sounds and sights of the street outside. As you can see, there are still plenty of decorating choices to make, even though at first glance the palette seems so narrow.

Furniture can be as battered as you want – the distressed finish of the wood will merely accentuate the textural qualities of the room. But that is not to say you must opt for cheap and cheerful. Contemporary designers are producing wonderfully sculptural pieces of furniture in woods and veneers that could take centre stage in any scheme. On the other hand, buy a junk-shop piece that you can renovate yourself and place the most perfect glass vase of lemons on it, or a wicker basket filled with shiny pebbles.

The aim is to pare down your belongings, if possible, so that the eye is drawn to one or two objects of pure beauty – perhaps a vase that you

love, a collection of white china, some gleaming glass, or a bowl of shells. You should work with naturals to produce an interior that is uncluttered, serene and has a sort of Zen-like beauty. Take inspiration from traditional Japanese homes, where interiors are of the utmost simplicity – wooden floors, a rolled bed, bamboo screens – but which include one object of beauty on which to meditate, perhaps a single glorious flower or a perfect piece of pottery. Followers of feng shui will recognize some of these references: in such a space it is believed that energy can flow freely, allowing life to be more creative and fulfilling.

The Final Result

The Bread and Butter colours are for people who value the spiritual as well as the material. They send out a message that your home is for you, not to impress those who might happen to visit. They demand that you choose every possession with care, but reward you with a sense of calm and serenity. They are about recognizing the really important things in life and surrounding yourself with them.

In Western society this is also the most contemporary of colour schemes, although the philosophy

behind it is thousands of years old and familiar throughout the Eastern world. It might not be practical to turn your entire home over to this style of decoration immediately, but every home could benefit from having at least one room that is a calm, inviting and sensual example of the naturals palette.

In my own living room
I have used polished
plaster walls, a limestone
floor, wood furniture and
fur throws to build up
a scheme that is rich in
layers and textures.

café au lait
and mocha

No-colour naturals are filled with the most subtle variations of
tone, which are as exciting and addictive as other more brilliant
shades. Think stone, wood, wheat. Think of rocks against bare earth
and reeds along a river. Conjure up memories of a country walk in
autumn and that moment when you reach the brow of a hill and
see the richness of the landscape laid out before you. Natural
colours – like the ones used in my own living room – are wonderfully easy to work with because you can layer so many ingredients
in a room and be confident that they will not fight for attention.

Right: One of the key pieces for me was this wonderful ammonite with its ridges and curves. Organic shapes can give so much inspiration – I have used the fossil to emphasize the importance of texture.

At first glance, you might think my living room has no right to be making an appearance in a book about colour. Colour suggests flamboyance, extroversion and boldness. But, of course, that is only part of the story. Colour can be infinitely varied and subtle, as that walk along Camber Sands (see page 18) always reminds me. In a room with generous proportions and good natural light, you too could take inspiration from natural ingredients containing masses of texture. A large fossil ammonite, for example, makes a wonderful starting point when putting together a room influenced by stony colours.

You don't need a particular type of home to make use of naturals – they can work as well in the country as in the city, and are certainly not dependent on period architectural features. All you need is the confidence to work with colours that, on their own, might not look very special at all. Their dynamism comes into play as they are juxtaposed with each other.

Texture, more than colour, can be the driving force. First decide how you are going to translate this on to the walls – perhaps with creamy Italian plaster stucco. If you think you need to break up the walls, create an imaginary dado line (see opposite);

Right: A small amount of black can go a long way – here I used black slubby silk and plain linen to make banner-style drapes for the windows. Black gives definition to this room, preventing it from becoming too buttery.

Left: Even in a room that is based around naturals, it is important to have one or two pieces that are strong in colour and so bring the scheme together – the brown of this leather chair becomes an anchor for the other shades.

layering texture

My own living room, particularly the sofa, is a perfect example of how lots of different textures can help to build up colour. In your own home, start with the walls, making a distinct contrast between matt and gloss. Then introduce fur, linen, silk, stone, twigs, or any other object that your fingers long to touch. The key to using texture lies in contrast: velvet will look even more velvety when placed next to a shiny surface, such as glass or steel; similarly, polished wood will have more impact when placed near a very coarse fabric.

Left: Because the natural world is so influential in my living room, I introduced ingredients such as these dried sticks to emphasize the connection. Simplicity and harmony are the key to using the neutral 'colours' with conviction.

Right: The important thing when designing a room is to continue the theme right down to the accessories. It is juxtaposition of texture that creates the visual interest – as here with stone, wood and fur.

Left: The organic shapes of these ceramic pots and jars touched a nerve with me when I first began designing my living room – I sprayed one of them black to give it an ethnic look.

this allows you to use one paint technique above it and solid colour below. You can accentuate the textural theme by having matt paint below the dado which will look sensational against a highly polished, almost mirrored, surface of the upper area. Don't choose colours that will fight: dove grey is the perfect companion to the clotted cream of polished plaster.

Cream will always work in a room such as this, but there is a danger that it will do so too well and the walls will disappear into the floor. That is why pure white on skirting boards and woodwork is essential; it lifts the other colours and creates some definition. Keep the skirting as deep as possible so that it almost frames the walls. Without that touch of white, the scheme might be in danger of looking too muted and restrained.

Black has a similar role to play. A little touch of black in the room – even if only on a fire surround – has a graphic quality that draws attention to the other shades. However, don't overdo it: none of the colours should shout for attention over the others.

Matt and shiny, hard and soft– these qualities are the core of the textural theme and can go in any direction: a mirrored chimney breast, fur throws over the sofa, African-inspired pots, a splintery wooden Buddha or a distressed coffee table from India. Also look for ways of leading the eye through the room to the walls: wrought-iron furniture and accessories are an excellent way of doing this as they have a sort of transparent quality.

It would ruin the whole effect to introduce any vivid colours as accents. Chocolate brown is about as far as you should go, but this can be used in fairly large quantities. A studded leather chair, for example, adds weight to a no-colour scheme and also accentuates the textural theme. You might like to add a suede cushion. Even the smallest amount of more definite colour would distract the eye and take the attention away from the layers of texture.

A café au lait and mocha room like this is perfect if, like me, you value calmness and serenity in your home. Where better for a colour enthusiast to flop down and recharge her batteries?

polished plaster effect

The subtle textured surface on the upper walls of Linda's living room is quite easy
to create, and you don't need the skills of a professional plasterer to achieve it.
With your chosen shade of stucco plaster (we used Full Fat Cream from Ray Munn),
a trowel and a little patience your walls will take on a beautiful lustre.

1 Mark off the dado line with low-tack masking tape. Paint the wall colour below the dado line with emulsion paint in your chosen colour.

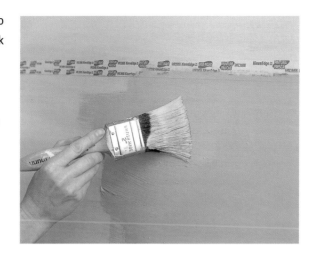

2 Once the paint has dried, reposition the masking tape, aligning the top edge of it with crisp line of the paint. Apply the first layer of plaster with a wet stainless steel trowel, tilting the bevelled edge of it at an angle of about 30 degrees. Skim the plaster on in a smooth, thin layer, completely covering the wall above the dado. The plaster should be no more than 2mm thick. Allow to dry.

3 Once the plaster is dry, looking matt and pale, apply a second layer of plaster on top just as described in step 2. Concentrating on an area of about 1 metre square, rework the wet plaster with a dry trowel so that the surface becomes polished. The more pressure you put against the trowel as you polish, the more lustre you will get. As it dries out, the plaster takes on a mottled finish.

The freshness and
simplicity of this youthful
sitting room take their
inspiration from the
nearby coast-line of the
Gower peninsula.

sea-grey

cobalt and sand

Grey is not a colour that people are drawn towards naturally.
Perhaps they think it will be too cold and austere. Yet if you look
around at nature, you will find that grey can be very beautiful:
think of pebbles on the beach or the feathers of seabirds. What
makes grey work in the natural world is that it is often juxtaposed
with warmer shades: pebbles might be mottled with reds and
golds and feathers streaked with black. Take your cue from this
when using grey in decorating, as I have in this seaside-inspired
sitting room. Most greys actually contain quite a lot of magenta,
which makes them warmer than you might first think. You can
bring this out by choosing warm colours for the accent shades.

Above and opposite: Natural is again the key word, so accessories, such as this split-cane blind, have been kept very simple. Sky blue and ochre linen cushions reflect the seaside theme.

Above and right: With the sea as such a strong influence on this living room, it is not surprising that shells should make an appearance. This collection has been used to make a wonderful focal point and has beautiful muted colours within it.

Another advantage of grey is its versatility. It is the sort of colour that can become a backdrop for whatever you want to impose on a room, be it a cool look designed around many layers of blue, or a minimalist's delight when teamed with black. Alternatively, you could go down the more modern path with, for example, three walls painted in soft dove and one in chocolate brown or mauve for an exciting ontrast.

When designing a room inspired by the colours of the sea, grey captures the mood perfectly – this is Britain, after all, and the sea here is colder, wilder and more unpredictable than Mediterranean or tropical waters. However, if you want to use a wall colour that reflects the true nature of our coastline, you must be sure to do so in a room with good light, otherwise it might look very stark and unwelcoming. If the light is not so good, but you have set your heart on this colour scheme, look for a way of boosting the light artificially, perhaps with well-positioned spotlights.

mixing colours

Choosing paint colours from tiny sample squares means everyone gets it wrong at some time or other. If you do choose a shade that is too cold, don't panic. It is possible to add a slightly warmer shade containing lots of magenta; learn to trust your own instincts. Pour the two colours into a tray and keep mixing until you have the effect you want, but do keep a note of the proportions used as you must have enough paint to cover all the walls.

The most interesting aspect of paint is the way it changes colour according to how the light hits it. When using grey, you might find that one wall actually looks blue. This is part of its charm and can accentuate the idea of the sea constantly

Left: Natural wood shutters are the perfect window adornment to introduce into a sea-grey room, but they can be expensive to buy. We made these by slotting pieces of bamboo into plain pine frames.

Above: It is always a good idea to find objects that provide inspiration before you begin designing – here pebbles from the beach influenced my approach. Gather together your own still life of loved treasures and learn from them.

fluctuating. One word of caution: it is a good idea to choose off-white paint for the woodwork and ceiling because brilliant white will probably make the grey look too harsh.

To prevent a grey scheme looking too cold, an accent shade is needed. Using hot colours, such as oranges, ochres, or even a touch of red, is one way of warming up cool base shades. But if you want to continue with the seaside theme, you might prefer to use cobalt (bright blue). This is the perfect foil to grey, as the two colours come from the same family. Use it in a slightly textured paint finish, rather than as solid colour, so that it does not jump out at you too much.

Having a theme also gives you direction when choosing accessories: grey walls, blue furniture and sandy yellow cushions will have the effect of metaphorically leading the eye from the sea to the sky to the beach and back to the sea again. By

keeping all the colours soft and hazy, you will accentuate the peaceful nature of the room.

Texture is a key ingredient when using natural colours. Not only does it add visual interest, but it also creates a sensual atmosphere because the eye is drawn towards materials, such as shiny pebbles or rough wood, that fingers long to touch. It also adds another dimension to a living space, and accentuates the idea that decorating is about more than paint colours. As textural layers are built up, the grey will lose its coldness and become mellow. It is important to remember this effect when designing any colour scheme: you must put all the elements of a room together before you can judge how well a colour is working. The paint in the pot might look quite daunting, as if the room could end up looking colder than the North Sea, but it might still be an excellent base for bringing many other ingredients together.

Left: Bleached bones are not everyone's choice as an accessory, but when combined with cacti for textural contrast they make a wonderful addition to a room so rich in natural references.

Right: Look closely at the wonderful textural detail in the surface of this wooden sideboard – distressed furniture is ideal for neutral schemes because its imperfections add interest. Old glass bottles and pebbles continue the flotsam and jetsam theme.

mirrored pebbles-on-a-roll

The polished floorboards in this sitting room are a beautifully warm colour, which is echoed to great effect in the pebbled border under the coving. The mirrored insets reflect the blues and greys in the room, helping to link the various textures and colours together.

1 Spread out the pebbles-on-a-roll (a pond liner available from aquatic centres) with the plastic backing uppermost. Using a pencil, measure out regularly spaced squares along the centre of the sheet, each one about 8cm square. (You'll need to calculate how many you need for the dimensions of your room.) Use a sharp craft knife to cut out the squares.

2 Cut a large mirror tile into strips 8cm wide. To do this, score the face of the mirror once with the rotary cutter held against a steel edge. Use the snapper part of the cutter to break the glass along the scored line.

3 Use a panel adhesive to stick the pebbles-on-a-roll into the required position on the wall. Use the same adhesive to glue the mirrors into the cut-out squares. CAUTION: Beware sharp edges when cutting mirror tiles, and wear safety goggles to protect your eyes from flying pebbles.

This tented dining room
with its creamy drapes
and aubergine edging looks
the ultimate in chic and
elegance. Incredibly it was
achieved with inexpensive
unlined dust sheets.

ivory
aubergine and white

Natural colours include off-whites, creams, greys, stones and taupes. They create a calm, restful atmosphere – a cocoon from the outside world. Cream is the warmest of the natural shades, which is why it remains perennially popular. Its attraction lies not only in its versatility – cream can work with just about any colour imaginable – but also in the mood it creates. Cream means under-stated elegance; it has a classic appeal which few other colours can emulate. The idea in this sumptuous dining room, designed by Graham Wynne, is to create a base on to which other stronger colours can be added.

Above: White and black are
used to give an edge to the
scheme – here pictures
with white mounts and
black frames play an
important part in anchoring
the look together.

There is nothing, however, to say that you are
restricted to paint for supplying colour. Lining
the walls with fabric, for instance, means that you
achieve all-round colour and also introduce
texture. Fabric is an instant way of changing the
colour of a room, as all you need are sheeting,
battens, staples and binding tape. Be careful,
though, when fixing battens near light switches and
electrical sockets. There may be cables behind the
plaster. To be extra safe, glue the wood in those
areas. Fabric is also ideal for covering walls in poor
condition because it does away with the weeks of
preparation. If you line the ceiling, too, you will find
that the effect is rather like being in an exclusive
and intimate marquee. Having started with such a
textural statement, you can continue the theme by
adding shiny chintz as a border, which makes an

Right: Shiny chintz in
strong aubergine was
chosen for the chair
covers – this contrasts
well colour-wise with the
cream of the lined walls,
and also provides textural
contrast against the matt
of the dust sheets.

light fantastic

Good lighting is essential in all rooms, but is absolutely crucial in a scheme where you are using swathes of fabric or a very textured wall finish. A simple overhead light will flatten the effect and therefore deaden it, so you must introduce lighting that will accentuate the design. Halogen uplighters are perfect because they bounce light off the ceiling and down the walls, thus bathing a room in a seductive glow.

excellent contrast to the roughness of sheeting.

You will certainly need to create some sort of textural interest if you are to avoid ending up with an old-fashioned magnolia scheme. You could do this by using a paint finish to bring in visual interest, or by using rough plaster to give the colour more depth.

If you want naturals to look punchy, you will need a strong accent colour. Aubergine is perfect because it punctuates all the creaminess and gives the room direction, but it is about as far as you can

Right: The dining table is an ingenious design – made from roofing joists which were limed. The flower-adorned table settings were chosen for their neutral tones.

stretch the naturals palette. Other suitable choices would be chocolate brown, pigeon grey or slate black. Black is a very dynamic colour when used with intense shades such as aubergine. You don't need much of it to make an impact: curtain poles, picture frames or occasional pieces of furniture are ideal ways of introducing it into a scheme. The theme of light and dark can then be picked up around the room.

White, too, is a surprisingly strong colour when teamed with naturals. As with black, it can be used in small but effective ways – through picture mounts or flowers, for example. It gives an edge to the cream and, in its way, is just as dynamic as black, so use it sparingly for maximum effect. White refreshes a cream room and prevents the feeling of living in a butter pat. A touch of green

Above: The luxurious atmosphere comes from everything being wrapped in fabric – including the window seat, on which plump bolster cushions add an extravagant touch.

Right: The importance of flowers cannot be over-estimated within a room – these white lilies with their sharp green leaves punctuate the creaminess all around them. White flowers can be a truly dynamic choice.

also adds a welcome sharpness to a Bread and Butter scheme.

Aubergine, black and white are perfect key players against a cream backdrop. Together they create a look that is elegant, sophisticated and nocturnal – ideal for a dining room that is more likely to be used at night than during the day. However, lighting is very important: it must be well positioned to highlight the texture of the walls and to distinguish between the more subtle shades.

Naturals are not synonymous with minimalism, where everything must be pared down for effect. Certainly the cluttered look is not appropriate, but neither is the puritanical. Dark furniture would be far too intrusive in such a sensual setting, so it is important to keep everything pale. The easiest solution is to swathe furniture in fabric, thus

Above: Good lighting is crucial in any room, but perhaps even more so in one designed around neutrals: uplighters concealed by urns on plinths add a dramatic touch to this scheme.

echoing the design of the room. The feeling of everything being wrapped in colour is seductive and sensual – far more so than very solid pieces of furniture would be.

Having created a cocoon of soft colour, you must now be careful not to introduce too many other shades or you will detract from its impact. A cream room is the core of the naturals palette, but it can be the foil for other types of scheme, too. Teamed with richer accent colours – like those found in Wine Gums (see page 110) – it can take on a very different, more exciting character.

lining walls with fabric

Both exotic and opulent, Graham's tented effect in this elegant dining room is easy to achieve and requires very little in the way of DIY skills.

1 Start by fixing wooden battens around the room. Use long lengths of ordinary pine about 2.5cm wide and 1cm thick. Screw further battens into the walls to make a series of frames; you need to allow for doors, light switches, electrical sockets and other awkward areas, so you'll end up with a variety of rectangular and square frames. The fabric will be attached to these.

2 Measure each rectangle in turn and cut a corresponding piece of fabric, including a generous 10cm allowance all round. Fold under the raw edges and staple it on to the battens, starting at the top corner along the top edge. Pull the fabric tightly to the skirting batten, turn over the raw edges and staple into position. Do the verticals next, starting in the middle of one side and working first downwards and then upwards. Make sure you keep the tension even throughout.

3 Cut eight to twelve lengths of fabric, depending on the size of your room. These should be half the distance of the ceiling plus 1.5m. Fold under the raw edges and staple the fabric to the battens at the top of the walls. Rather than bringing the fabric taut across the ceiling, allow it to drape slightly for a tented effect. Tie the excess fabric into a knot in the centre of the room and secure with more staples.

sugared alm

onds

pastel shades

■

Imagine being transported into a Monet landscape – one of the water-lily paintings showing
the gardens of Giverny. I find myself in a haze
of blues, greens, pinks, yellows and lilacs with dots
of white here and there. There is sunlight and
water all around me, but I see them through a mist
so that the colours slide and blend into one
another. The warmth and softness is reminiscent
of the softest cashmere scarf. This is the gentle
romance of pastels.

For many years, the paint charts were dominated
by a range of colours described as 'Hints of ...' –
pale shades that were easy to assimilate into a
room. Sugared Almonds is my name for that same
group, but with far more strength. Imagine taking
a delicious colour, such as brilliant blue or post-box
red, then pouring milk into it so that it becomes
dense and opaque. For it is the addition of white
that gives these colours their opaqueness. Such
colours conjure up Continental images of pistachio
ice-cream, strawberry tarts and banana milkshake.
They also make me think of Italian cassatas, or
blueberry pie as the cream hits the fruit. They have
neither the harsh glare of summer nor the richness
of autumn, but are reminiscent of spring days.
The haziness they create is like looking at colours
through fine muslin or a light fog, and gives the
impression that walls are receding. This makes
Sugared Almond colours perfect for those dark and
dingy spaces where you want to create a feeling
of energy and light.

The emotions engendered by Sugared Almond
colours are calm and peaceful. They are ideal for
people who lead busy lives and who want to return
to spaces that soothe them. Pastels do not shout

and clash but, like that Monet landscape, wash over you, leaving you with a sense of peace. They have a classic appeal which will always have a place in our lives.

How to Use Pastels

What makes Sugared Almonds so popular is that they are very easy colours to live with – unassuming and suitable for any room. They are never going to shriek at you. Traditionally popular in bedrooms and bathrooms, they now have relevance throughout the whole house. For instance, they are ideal for living spaces where you want to merge one space into another and have a sense of continuity as you look through doors into adjacent rooms. They also lend themselves to the idea of being changed according to the seasons: loose covers, curtains, cushions and accessories can all be replaced with another set, yet the backdrop remains the same.

As pastels create a plain canvas, there is a danger that they could look boring. The secret is to introduce other accent colours to bring in the 'oomph'. Imagine, for example, pale lilac walls. Now add a burnt orange sofa and other hot-coloured

accessories. The lilac will take on a new dynamism with such strong companions.

Pastels are simple colours to play around with – you can combine them to your heart's content. There is no need to be restricted by numbers – you could use five or six of these shades in a room and get away with it because they are all light tones which are easy on the eye. You could choose one

colour for the walls, another for the skirting board, a third for the upholstery, a fourth for the curtains and another for key accessories. Since you can do so much with colour, texture plays a smaller part than in other colour families. It also means that you can be braver about using pattern, and even introduce more than one without fear of them clashing madly. Take pattern up a notch – go that bit braver with it than you usually dare.

Blocks of colour on walls are the latest trend in interiors, fast replacing colour-washing, stencilling, dragging and the like. Sugared Almond shades are perfect for experimenting with in this way: try using one colour for three of the walls and another for the fourth. Or think about adding stripes in complementary shades – perhaps a silver stripe on ice blue walls (see page 60), or plaster pink on palest green. Combinations like these are very effective and the colours won't take your breath away as you put them on the wall.

These colours, however, do need good light, otherwise they can fade away into insignificance, or look stark and cold. But remember that light can change colours even within the same room: the living room I painted in Gower (see page 33) was

sea grey, yet at least one wall looked blue because of the light. I liked that effect, but a visitor would have been convinced that I had chosen two separate colours for the same room. Good artificial lighting for the evening is also crucial. Use halogen bulbs to bring warmth to these colours, particularly the blues, which will need a lot of magenta in them.

Ingredients

Working with the pastels palette means that you might be able to retain your existing carpet, as long as it isn't patterned with orange dots or brown swirls. If the carpet does have to go, take a look at the boards underneath: perhaps they could be painted or lime-washed to match the softness of the walls. Alternatively, you could make a really strong statement by having, say, black floors with pastel walls. I've actually tried this (see page 75) and, interestingly, the black didn't dominate at all.

Woodwork should be cream rather than white because our northern light responds much better to slightly muddy shades than pure ones. Brilliant white is a very dominant colour, which can leave surrounding shades looking rather dirty. As far as furniture is concerned, anything is acceptable, from

very distressed pieces to ultra-modern ones. Wood, metal, stone, glass – all these suit a calming pastel environment. I like the eclectic look best – a brave combination of old and new, such as a carved Indian table with a highly modern ceramic bowl on it. This Sugared Almonds look can be a great deal more flexible than other colour families.

Curtains can be floaty and pretty, and because pattern is a plus in this colour scheme they are an ideal way of introducing it. Similarly, you can also introduce lots of accessories – cushions, throws,

rugs and so on – because everything works well together. You can also use very bold accessories, such as heavy picture frames, chunky candlesticks and over-sized pots, with this sort of colour base.

In the Bread and Butter section the idea was to pare down possessions and achieve a pure, almost austere environment. With pastels shades the problem is knowing when to stop adding accessories because you could end up with a room that is very chintzy with too many bits and pieces to have any real impact.

The Final Result

Sugared Almonds are perfect for people who appreciate a restful environment to return to each evening. They do not demand the purist approach of the neutrals or the courage of the vivids, so are an excellent halfway house for those who want to work with colour yet do not want something that will yell and scream. Sugared Almonds all work well together, and make the perfect canvas on which to introduce existing items of furniture and well-loved bits and pieces.

Horizontal stripes in
shades of blue emphasize
the generous proportions
of this airy living room.
Mirrored tiles and silver
accessories highlight the
modern look.

ice-blue
denim and silver

Ice-blue is the sort of Sugared Almonds shade that many people
long to use, but are scared of in case it makes their home look
too cold. But for those of us who love wintry shades, it can be
the perfect choice, particularly when combined with silver. I used
it in this *Changing Rooms* living room for an extremely contemporary look. As with other colours, it is what you complement it
with and how much available light there is that makes all the
difference. In fact, blue works well with many other colours:
cream if you want to warm it, white if you want to cool it, grey
if you want to echo the sea, black if you want to give it an edge.

painting floorboards

Floors are terribly important in decorative schemes, but are one of the most expensive areas to deal with. If you are lucky enough to have decent floorboards, think about stripping and painting them. By using just one coat of floor paint – matt emulsion would do – you can achieve a colour-washed effect with the grain of the wood showing through. Then all you need to do is apply a protective varnish on top.

Opposite and below:
Wintry colours can look
cold – luckily there is
enough natural light here.

The beauty of Sugared Almond shades is that they are so restful. A blue like the one used here shows off a fine room perfectly and is a joy to step into because it creates such an atmosphere of calm. Blue is a very evocative colour, bringing to mind sky, sea and far-away hills. These associations also tend to make it the most meditative of colours.

A room with natural southerly light and good proportions is the ideal space in which to use blue to dramatic effect. If you do use it as a wall colour, remember that the woodwork shade will make all the difference. Brilliant white will accentuate the iciness of the blue, so choose creamy white to soften the effect.

As pale blue is quite a cold colour, you need to use other materials to warm it up. A natural wooden floor, for example, can be glazed in a sandy shade to lighten it. Natural wooden shutters are ideal at the windows. Use soft, textured fabrics,

Left: Neutrals, such as this pale coffee table, blend well with the wintry shades.

Right: The unusual candle stand was made out of chunks of reclaimed wood which were then glued together. A square candle echoes the shapes.

such as linen, calico and muslin, to layer the scheme. The idea is that none of the colours should jar: try to create a space that is calming and liberating.

Sometimes Sugared Almonds can lack substance and texture, so look for ways of breaking up the wall space. Pictures are one way of doing this, but applied decoration is another. A much warmer shade of blue, such as denim, can be used to punctuate the paler shade. If you are working within a big space, it is very important to create character; one way of doing this is to paint wide horizontal stripes of flat colour around the walls. You can then colour-wash the lower third of the walls by dragging the warmer shade down over the pale blue to create more interest. Horizontal stripes can be used to play visual jokes as they invariably make a space seem bigger than it really is.

You will now need some sort of accent colour to break up the two shades of blue. Metallic silver is the fashionable choice of the moment and looks fabulous against blues of all description. Use it to create a slim horizontal stripe that punctuates the wall like a traditional dado rail. Another choice would be to team the soft blue with other sugary colours, such as pale greens, pinks and yellows, but the overall effect will not be so exciting as the addition of silver. In a small space, you might want to bring in more punch. If so, stronger colours, such as burnt orange, blueberry or blackcurrant, can be used to draw the eye.

In a room with two functions, such as a living-cum-dining room, you can use colour and applied decoration to distinguish between the two areas, as we have done here. For example, choose stripes for one end of the room and squares for the other; that way the two ends of the room can be unified both in colour and geometry, while still retaining their own characters. It is also a way of breaking up the colour on the walls, which might lack depth if painted flat in one light shade. Bear in mind that you don't have to use this decoration at the same height each time; it is quite acceptable to bring the eye towards the dado height in one area and up to the coving in another. In fact, this emphasizes the generous proportions of a room.

Blues and silver together achieve a cool, contemporary look that perfectly suits a room with fine architectural details, good natural light and generous proportions. You don't need a lot of other colours fighting for attention in a Sugared Almonds room, so use no-colour naturals to retain a harmonious atmosphere.

Left: Mirrors accentuate the metallic finish on the walls. Above the fireplace, mirrored tiles have been used to frame an existing mirror and give it more prominence. Bright blue glass adds zing.

painted wall stripes

Geometric shapes, such as stripes, might seem rather tricky to make, but they're not. The secret of success, even for the unsteadiest hand, is masking tape.

1 Paint the walls with your chosen base colour. When dry, use a pencil and spirit level to mark out the first stripes. These should be broad – at least 30cm deep. Stick low-tack masking tape along these lines, then paint in the second colour.

2 Once dry, remove the tape. At shoulder height, and again using a spirit level, mark out another stripe; this should cut one of the paler stripes in half. Apply masking tape again. Below this line, begin to apply the colour-wash – a diluted version (1:1 paint and water) of the first stripe colour. You are aiming for a cloudy effect over the paler base colour. When dry, remove the tape.

3 Mark out a narrow stripe (about 5cm deep) above the colour-washed stripe, using a pencil and spirit level. Apply a double row of masking tape above and below this stripe because when the chrome paint is sprayed on it tends to disperse more than ordinary paint. (Chrome spray paint is available in the Odds & Ends range by Plastikote.)

My own bedroom is a
seductive blend of plaster
pink, soft green and
shocking pink. Hand-drawn
calligraphy on the walls
adds a romantic touch.

camomile
fennel and coral

The idea of a pink room is one that has many people reaching for
the smelling salts. It conjures up images of Barbie dolls, candy
floss, sticks of rock and little girls' boudoirs. Pink is not a natural
choice if you want to achieve a sophisticated and contemporary
look, yet stop for a moment and address that prejudice. Chances
are that you have eaten in restaurants or visited shops where
pink has been a key colour. The 1980s took the idea of pink and
turned it on its head, with many commercial designs exploiting
Italian-style plaster pink. The 1990s have continued the trend with
increasingly chic ways of combining pink with other colours – grey,
black, cream and green, for example – to achieve numerous looks.

Yet all too often pink is rejected because of its sugary associations.

It is a colour that has seen many fashions come and go. We think of pink as a little girl's colour, but for the Victorians it was a colour for little boys. So much for sexual stereotyping! Still, I have to admit that when we were looking for a pink room to photograph for this book it took a while for it to dawn on me that my own bedroom was pink. Somehow I had never consciously admitted that the rough plastered look I had chosen did indeed have a rosy glow. Bedrooms and bathrooms are the obvious places to try out pink, but in fact it has great relevance as a living-room or dining-room colour because it shares many of the same qualities of cream – it is so warm, welcoming and enveloping.

Pink is also surprisingly versatile and can work as well in a small, dark room as a large, airy one. It doesn't demand the same quantity of light as blues and greys – in fact, candlelight alone can give it a fabulously seductive look. When you move away from the baby pinks with which it is most associated, and into the denser shades, you realize that it is actually a very sexy colour. It is also ideal for period houses, as pink has a long and influential connection with country house decoration. Look through any of the historical paint ranges now available and you will find muddy shades of pink that suit our northern light perfectly.

If you are considering using pink, bear in mind that it works better as a textured surface than as flat colour. Like red, it has attitude. Try a rough

plaster or colour-washed look where another warm shade – cream is ideal – breaks up the pinkness of the scheme. Soft green is also an excellent partner to pink, as it is pretty without being twee. Not all the Sugared Almond shades would work so well; you need a colour with a little punch that will not be submerged by the base colour.

You now need an accent colour that can also hold its own against pink. If you have used a sugary pink on the walls, you could try using shocking pink or coral to give it even more zing. Black is also an excellent choice because it brings definition to a room, but you might find it too stark. Charcoal grey is an excellent in-between shade – strong enough to take on the pink, yet not so strong that it tires the eyes. It gives sophistication to a scheme that might otherwise be in danger of becoming too girly.

Right: Large diamond motifs on the walls add interest and introduce colour variation. The paint finish is intentionally imperfect.

Above: The furniture has been given a slightly aged look – this suits the character of the room better than natural wood.

Right: Decorative accessories such as the mirror, the mound of scatter cushions and the bedcover suit the prettiness of the room.

distressing furniture

Breaking up the colour on walls and furniture is very easy and gives a wonderfully textural finish. Here, cream emulsion was applied to the furniture, then, when it had dried, soft green emulsion was painted on top. Oak furniture polish was then rubbed into the paint, giving it an uneven quality, as it removed some of the paint, and allowed first the cream and then some of the wood grain to show through. Apply the polish with a cloth for a subtle look, or wire wool for a more obvious one.

Don't introduce too many other colours to a pink room: simplicity is the key to keeping it chic. A slightly distressed finish on furniture is ideal, though, as it echoes the textural theme on the walls. Floor, window treatments and accessories should all accentuate the mood of harmony and restfulness. Cream is one way of doing this; naturals are another. You don't want too intense a range of colours or the result will be rather cloying and sickly. When pink works well, there is nothing quite like it for creating a soft and sensual atmosphere.

plaster effect and calligraphy

There's a definite Italian influence on the walls of Linda's bedroom. The aged plaster look was actually created with the simplest of paint techniques. The ornate cursive script applied on top completed the historic feel of the room.

1 Create the basic plaster effect by painting the walls with a flat colour and then applying a top coat of paler paint. This will give a slightly mottled appearance.

2 Using a pencil, spirit level and a long rule or length of timber, mark out the diamond shapes on the wall; they should extend from floor to picture rail. Paint in the diamonds using a thinned white emulsion (2:1 paint to water) and an almost dry brush so that the finished surface has a scrubbed look.

3 Find a suitable piece of calligraphy, perhaps from old books or postcards. Enlarge and photocopy the script on to clear film at a copy bureau, then place it on an overhead projector and project it on to the wall. Trace off the projected script using an artist's brush and thinned grey emulsion paint. Alternatively, enlarge the calligraphy and use carbon paper to transfer the script to the walls. Don't worry if the lettering is slightly wobbly – this can actually enhance the effect.

Milky mauve is a wonderfully restful shade in a bedroom. Painting the ceiling the same colour as the walls unifies the room and creates an airy feeling.

lilac
blueberry and silver

Lilac is soft and gentle, perfect for a room where you want a sense of calm. In decoration terms, it has been much ignored in recent years – perhaps because it has traditionally been seen as an overtly feminine colour. Happily, people are now recognizing what a very versatile colour it is. In a small space, a stronger shade, such as purple, would be too heavy and oppressive. The idea of Sugared Almonds is to take the more powerful colour and then add white, as if milking down blueberry purée to mousse, so that it becomes a more acceptable shade for the space. I used lilac here to lighten up a dark front bedroom.

Left: Before tackling the bedroom decoration, it was important to deal with the problem of clothes storage. An 'invisible' wall was created to conceal everyday clutter.

Right: Horizontal stripes are an important motif in this small bedroom because they help to create an illusion of space. Silver is the perfect accent colour to lilac and has been used on the bedhead, furniture, cushions and the curtains.

Right: Overscaling the
bedhead introduces height
into the room and tricks
the eye into thinking the
space is larger than it
really is. Silver edging
adds glamour.

Bear in mind that you must have good light when using shades of lilac. If the windows are small and the natural light poor, you should consider introducing extra artificial light, such as a circle of spotlights. Halogen lighting is best as it brings out the true nature of colours. Without good lighting, a pale colour scheme will have only a quarter of its impact, so make sure you're happy with yours before you begin.

Having created a restful environment, it would be a mistake to introduce colours that might disturb its serenity. A good way of introducing a touch of visual excitement is to paint one wall in a slightly stronger shade than your Sugared Almond choice – say, smoky blue against lilac – to give it more edge. To trick the eye into thinking that a space is wider than it is, you could paint a horizontal line around the room. This should be very subtle: you want to create more definition than the flat colour gives, not slice the room in two. In a bigger room with better light, however, you might think about introducing other colours – a warm orange, perhaps, or a dark blackberry, depending on the mood you want to create.

Black is a dynamic ingredient to introduce to a Sugared Almond room. It might seem a surprising

Right: Accessories should be chosen for what they contribute to a room – lavender complements the lilac walls perfectly and has the advantage of a wonderful scent.

choice against such soft colours, but having created the right atmosphere, it is important to introduce something that will punctuate the room and give it more definition. Natural flooring or pale carpet are safe choices, but might look too enveloping and bland. You could introduce black either through flooring, which will prevent the walls from disappearing into the skirting board, or through furniture. Interestingly, black looks fabulous against lilac – rather chic and French, like something you would see in a Parisian apartment. If you want to be adventurous, you could take the idea one step further with some sort of applied decoration in black on the walls.

Highlighting colours are crucial in any scheme. Silver is the perfect choice for lilac and black

because it blends in rather than shouting for attention. In fact, the combination of lilac, black and silver is a very sophisticated and dynamic one. It is quite different from the chintzy way that lilac is so often used with pale greens, yellows and pinks, and shows what a flexible colour it actually is.

As with all the Sugared Almond shades, the contribution of the naturals should not be overlooked. They create another subtle layer of visual interest, but will not disrupt the harmonious feeling in a room. This makes them ideal for accessories and extra pieces of furniture.

If decorating a bedroom, texture should also be carefully considered. The idea of bedrooms is to be as sensual and glamorous as possible; silk, satin and scent are just three of the ingredients that can make all the difference. The combination of rough and smooth has a relevance to the Sugared Almonds palette, too. Meanly proportioned rooms benefit from textural contrasts because these distract attention from the overall space and focus it on specific items.

Colour can be layered in small spaces to create something really special. Any of the Sugared Almond colours – primrose yellow, dusty pink, soft green – can be given strength by a touch of black and a stimulating accent colour.

using bold colours

In a small room with restricted natural light, you might feel you have no choice but to use a muted Sugared Almonds shade. But if you long for more intense colour, consider painting a feature wall in a much darker colour: this lilac bedroom actually has one deep purple wall, which adds character. You can unify all the walls by running a stripe around the room, which visually holds the whole look together.

Left: It is interesting just how versatile a colour black is: a black vinyl floor is an unexpected touch here, but works brilliantly well with the lilac and adds an eye-catching edge to a scheme that might otherwise become insipid.

silver detailing on furniture

While silver might not be the first colour that springs to mind when you think of furniture, it certainly works a treat when set against the cool lilac of this bedroom and it is incredibly easy to recreate.

1 Prepare the chest of drawers by removing the handles and then cleaning and sanding it. Apply a coat of white wood primer so that it is ready for painting. Now draw a circle on the front of the chest, making sure it is positioned centrally. To do this, tap a nail into the centre front and tie a piece of string to it. Tie a pencil to the other end of the string, making sure that when the string is taut, the circle will be of the correct diameter.

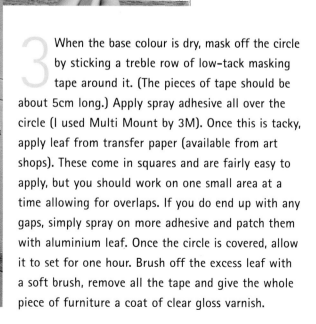

2 Apply two coats of emulsion base colour around the circle.

3 When the base colour is dry, mask off the circle by sticking a treble row of low-tack masking tape around it. (The pieces of tape should be about 5cm long.) Apply spray adhesive all over the circle (I used Multi Mount by 3M). Once this is tacky, apply leaf from transfer paper (available from art shops). These come in squares and are fairly easy to apply, but you should work on one small area at a time allowing for overlaps. If you do end up with any gaps, simply spray on more adhesive and patch them with aluminium leaf. Once the circle is covered, allow it to set for one hour. Brush off the excess leaf with a soft brush, remove all the tape and give the whole piece of furniture a coat of clear gloss varnish.

ding

I am dressing up for a night at the opera. On goes the shocking pink evening gown, the sequinned shoes, the scarlet lipstick, the peacock blue silk wrap, the glittering jewels. With colour like that, I should wow them in the aisles. Think summer pudding. Think Christmas tree lights. Think Disneyland. This is full colour at its most saturated.

Such vivid colour – Moroccan blue, Chinese yellow, Grecian pink and Irish green – is not for the faint-hearted. Many people don't like it at all (as *Changing Rooms* can testify) because it is so uncompromising. If it were a food, it would be summer pudding oozing with crushed raspberries and strawberries and crowned with a sprig of the freshest mint. In nature it evokes the most crimson of roses, the bluest delphinium, a whole flowerbed of red hot pokers on a scorching summer's day. It is full of passion and vibrancy, and will shout for attention as you walk through the door. You can love it or hate it, but you certainly can't ignore it.

From a design point of view, vivid colour is fantastic to use because you can completely change the character of a space with nothing but a pot of paint. The paint, however, won't come cheap: the best colours are often the most expensive because they contain so much more pigment than other colours. To my mind, though, they are worth every penny.

These colours are full of emotion and energy, which will transfer to you, so be warned! They bring out the best in extrovert, confident and exuberant people who like to wake up in the morning and be fired with enthusiasm for the new day. They demand that you live up to them and enjoy their boldness, and are incredibly rewarding when done well.

There is no point even considering this vivid family of colours if your wardrobe has nothing in it but black and oatmeal. But if you have fiery red, punchy purple or gutsy orange in there, you might well love a Summer Pudding colour scheme. If you are even toying with the idea, you probably have the sort of personality that could cope with it.

How to Use Vivid Colours

You have to start by really wanting colour of vivid intensity. Then you need to search for the one that really turns you on: back to that still life you created (see page 9) to find out which shade is best for you. The vivid palette is about wall colour, solid colour, giving a room an instant face-lift; it is not about one red sofa or a green cupboard. The power of this palette comes from being surrounded by colour in every direction. As the walls reflect colour on to each other, they take on even more vibrancy.

You will need plenty of light, particularly of the natural sort, otherwise vivid rooms can seem austere by day. For night-time, you should think carefully about what artificial light to introduce.

Use halogen lighting, if possible, because it creates a cleaner, crisper effect, and install a dimmer switch so that you have a certain amount of control. Candles can also be very effective in strongly coloured rooms, particularly in the evenings. In a dramatic-looking dining room, for instance, candle-light can add another mood-enhancing dimension to the overall scheme.

You might think that vivids are suitable only in large rooms, but you would be wrong. A very small room can be given character by painting it in one really dramatic shade – midnight blue perhaps, or even black. Period homes with wonderful architectural detailing can take colour in big doses, but so can modern architecture.

Because its dramatic effect lies in solid colour, the vivid palette does not need texture on the walls. However, you must prepare thoroughly to make the surface as smooth and unblemished as possible before paint is applied. If you skimp on preparation, the eye will focus on blemishes and miss some of the impact of the colour itself.

To use vivids well does require skill, as they work best in rooms that are layered with colour: walls are the starting point and core to their success, but there must be a feeling that everything else has followed on from them. You should not tone down the furnishings to lessen the impact of the walls, but build them up to increase that impact. The look is breezy and confident.

Ingredients

As far as floors are concerned, anything goes in a vivid colour scheme. Natural floors, be they covered in parquet, paint or sisal, work beautifully. Limed or bleached floors would not be gutsy enough, but some carpet shades in bold colours such as royal red, midnight blue or black would be fine. However, such true colours do not come cheap.

Windows must be dramatic. Coloured banners

that create huge blocks of colour look sensational in a bold room (see page 27), as do more traditional curtains made from masses of fabric such as tapestry, paisley or damask. However, vivid rooms are not the place for a clashing pattern – there is quite enough going on already. Nor would the prettiness of flowered swags and tails be appropriate. You could opt for very modern or very traditional windows, but a smart tailored look is the one to aim for. Summer Pudding colours are very theatrical and the windows should echo that.

When the walls are so vivid, you need to carry the effect throughout the rest of the room. If your sofa is beige, for example, you will have to add huge cushions in punchy colours to make it look the part. A simple wooden table will need an exotic runner across it. Plain curtains will need to be edged with dramatic pompoms. Think of the exuberance of Brighton Pavilion and you are halfway there.

You could use any style of furniture you want, as long as it is bold enough to sit happily in such a setting. Antique pieces in dark woods will look wonderful, as would modern designs in graphic black. Accessories are crucial: mirrors are a must

because reflective surfaces look sensational in dramatic settings. I love to combine matt finishes with gloss ones for impact, perhaps by just painting a metallic varnish over a matt paint. The idea is to create multiple layers by adding furnishings and accessories. Fabrics are very important: throws, rugs, cushions and windows treatments all combine to accentuate richness and character. Flowers are also an integral part of this scheme – the stronger and more dramatic the colour, the better.

The importance of light, both natural and artificial, has already been mentioned, but in a vivid environment with many rich ingredients the presence of light and dark adds a new twist. Like an Old Master working on a great painting, you slowly build up your still life, taking care over each colour, but it is the use of light that will decide how great a painting it really is.

The Final Result

The interesting thing about the vivid palette is that you can choose either the historic route or the modern. It is easy to forget that the faded shades we see in historic houses were once brilliant colours. If you need convincing, visit Sir John Soane's Museum in Lincoln's Inn Fields, London, and see how he combined yellows, blacks and reds to sumptuous effect over 200 years ago. Before that, the Elizabethan palette was also very strong. And centuries before that, the Egyptians were showing how colour could be used to dynamic effect.

There's nothing new about decorating with

colour, but it takes courage to use it if you're used to living in a more muted environment. But look around you – lots of people have kicked magnolia out the door and are finding the confidence to live with vibrant colours again. This is not about wanting to shock, but it is about creating beauty and interest through boldness. The Summer Pudding colour scheme is not difficult to carry off, but if you are timid, you could always start by painting your downstairs loo first: the dynamic result will guarantee a buzz of heady excitement that will set you off on even bigger and bolder experiments.

Vivid colours against
brilliant white transform
this basement sitting room
into a Manhattan-style
apartment, complete with
own modern artwork.

tutti-frutti
ice-cream

The excitement of the Summer Pudding palette suggests a room
that vibrates before your eyes. But, if you prefer, you can take a tip
from Laurence Llewelyn-Bowen and introduce brilliant splashes
of colour into your scheme while retaining a sense of calm.
It is all about percentages – how much of the wall space, floors
and furniture you impose colour on. Small areas of very intense
shades can be just as effective as covering whole walls with paint
– applied decoration today means allowing the imagination to
take a very free approach. The idea is to start with a crisp, clean
canvas, which is itself a dynamic partner to paint.

Below: Here the green of the apples contrasts beautifully with the bright pink fruit bowl – this could have been the starting point for the room's colour scheme. Remember always to look around you for inspiration when exploring colour combinations.

Above: Bands of intense colours are juxtaposed for maximum vibrancy. The white backdrop creates a frame around them, giving them even more prominence.

You could, for example, paint the walls white and then add cubes, stripes and circles in techno-rainbow shades – brilliant greens, pinks, yellows, reds, blues, whites, silver – in fact, anything you can lay your hands on. The beauty of this palette is that it doesn't matter if you place colours that scream and clash next to each other because proportionally they cover only a small part of the overall wall area. Just imagine you are creating a piece of modern art.

The finished result will certainly be fabulous.

The new trend in applied decoration is to use blocks of colour for effect, rather than techniques such as colour-washing, stencilling and sponging. The blocks can be scaled down so that you have lots of them rather than painting just one wall a slightly different shade from the other three. Use colours randomly: a symmetrical pattern would be a mistake as the eye would be led to the pattern rather than to the colours. If you are not sure you would have the courage to try painting the walls yourself, why not experiment with felt pens or art

Left: It takes confidence to create such a seemingly random effect as this. Each shade has been put next to one that makes it jump and jar. Squares of silver add another layer of interest and visual excitement.

paints on a piece of paper first?

Blocks of colour are perfect for a room that is small, dark or meanly proportioned because you can introduce a sense of order through the geometrical shapes. It is also ideal for modern houses where there might not be many architectural features to which the eye can be drawn. Not only does the pattern give masses of visual stimulation, but it also tricks the eye into thinking the room is bigger and taller than it actually is. This is partly because of the way the colours interact with white, which creates an impression of space around them.

Pure white has quite a different character from cream or magnolia. It demands attention, whereas the warmer versions become invisible. It is this dynamism that makes brilliant white the ideal blank canvas for vivid colours: it is not so much a backdrop as a frame for bright colours. In this respect, it is similar to black.

In a dark, low room white injects energy. Before applying it, though, the artificial lighting must be boosted, otherwise any white will look dingy. Well-positioned spotlights can really bring a space alive.

mixing colour families

What is interesting about the vivid Summer Pudding palette is the part that neutrals have to play. A room with a very strong colour statement on the walls does not need anything else shrieking for attention. Concrete, paving slabs and unpainted MDF create a harmonious look that does not fight with the stronger colours around it. These also add texture, which is important in a room full of brilliant, but flat colour.

Right: Neutrals are surprisingly effective in such a colour-driven room. This Perspex-and-stone table creates a visual joke as well as a focal point.

Left: A line of red cushions on the MDF seating makes a bold statement, accentuating the powerful feel of the room.

Below: Geometric shapes are the core of the scheme and have been used to frame features within the room as well as to bring in striking colour.

If you want to keep attention focused on the walls, you should ensure that floors, windows and furniture remain quiet and harmonious so that they will not attract attention. Some Summer Pudding schemes demand that every ingredient in a room is lit with colour, but naturals have a part to play in a room where a small but vigorous amount of colour is used. The floor, window treatment and furniture should be so harmonious that the eye is led only to the patches of colour on the walls, with nothing to interrupt the effect. Black furniture could be used, but this would look very stark against the white and would therefore be intrusive. Dark furniture would be entirely the wrong tone to sit happily with the Disneyland colours.

Rooms that make a striking statement with colour lose their edge if too cluttered, so you must be a purist to maintain the effect. Old newspapers, children's toys or kicked-off shoes ruin the serenity of a scheme. The approach is almost minimalist, but with the impact of several fabulous colours on top. You must, however, know when to stop. The blocks, stripes and circles are enough on their own: *trompe l'oeil* frames around them or anything more ornate would destroy their effect. That aside, the idea is a simple one and could easily be transported into your own home. Who said that all life is art?

painted squares

What a difference colours can make! Here Laurence's painted squares in bold Summer Pudding colours give a decidedly modern feel to the room.

1 Mark out a grid pattern of squares on the wall
   using a spirit level, pencil and ruler. The squares
   should be at least 14cm square. Fill in alternate
squares with emulsion or acrylic paint colours. You
don't have to use masking tape as none of the sides
can bleed into any other colours, but do so if it gives
you more confidence. Once these are dry, fill in the
other squares.

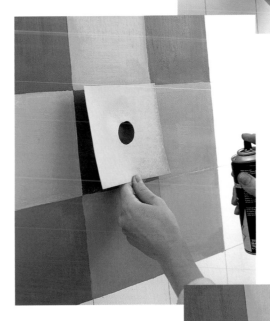

2 To add a silver
   spot to some of
   the squares, cut
a mask of the same
dimensions from stencil
card and cut a hole
approximately 3cm in
diameter in the centre.
Hold the mask lightly
away from the square
where you want the
spot and spray adhesive
through the hole (the
adhesive we used was
Multi Mount from 3M).

3 Once the glue
   becomes tacky,
   apply aluminium
leaf to the prepared spot
with your finger.

A dynamic combination of black, white and shocking pink transforms this bedroom into a far sexier boudoir. Aubrey Beardsley was the inspiration for the art nouveau motifs used on the floor and furniture.

fuchsia
blackcurrant and black

Hot colours are probably the most exciting of the Summer Pudding range. Their instant impact makes them a joy to use, as Laurence Llewelyn-Bowen found out when he designed this boudoir. Strong, vivid and absolutely uncompromising, they metaphorically take a room by the throat and force it into submission. Suffice it to say, they are not for the faint-hearted. They can be used to create wonderfully clashing schemes when placed next to other fiery tones, or take on a more sophisticated appearance by being placed next to black for dramatic effect.

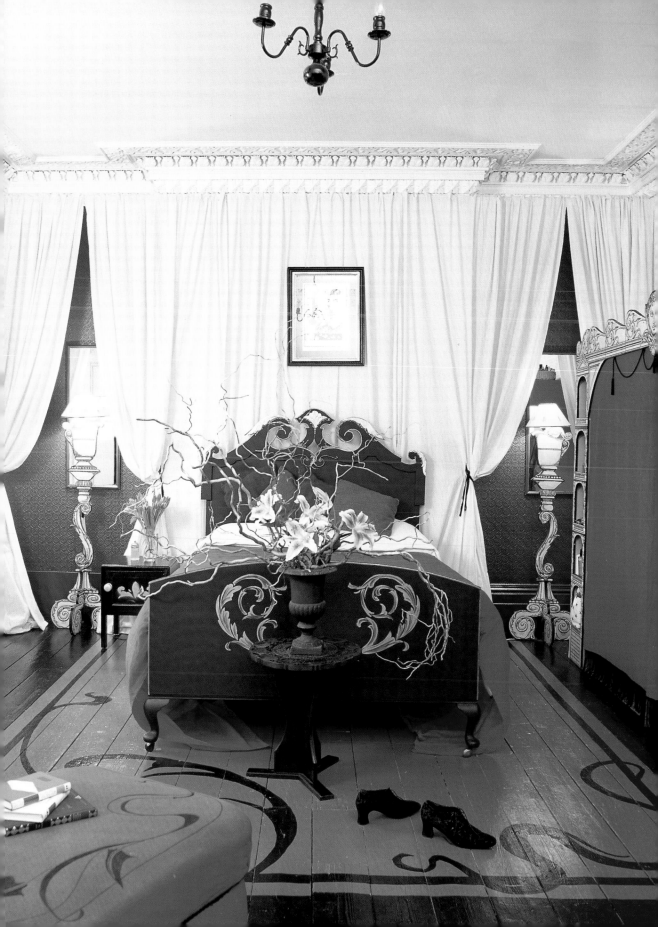

Above: The accessories such as the black-framed oval mirror and the silver candlesticks have been chosen for the period feel they bring to the room. The look is a pastiche on the 1890s, rather than a purist version.

Right: The *trompe l'oeil* rug on the floor makes dramatic use of the painted floorboards. It is an excellent way of adding interest when the budget will not allow you to carpet such a large area. The swirly Beardsley motif is echoed on the bed.

Right: The theatrical look of the room has been accentuated with this ornate bedhead made out of MDF. The white drapes behind make the perfect backdrop on which to project its graphic lines and bold colours.

If you are looking for a colour that will set a scheme alight, fuchsia does so perfectly. It is so vigorous that it creates a real sense of excitement against black. Interestingly, though, the pink takes over and the black becomes a frame for the more powerful colour. Few other shades would have the intensity to achieve this: emerald green, turquoise blue and imperial yellow (all from the Summer Pudding palette) would have the clarity required, but anything muddy would make black look sombre rather than chic.

Black and white are, of course, classic combinations, bringing to mind the elegance of Cecil Beaton, the nostalgia of old Hollywood films, or the graphic lines of Mary Quant dresses. In decorating terms, they are often associated with the minimalist approach, particularly when joined by grey, but there is no reason to be constrained by that because they offer all sorts of possibilities, as this dramatically sexy boudoir shows.

Black is a colour that people are often afraid of using because they think it might look too sombre

and funereal in the home. But it becomes fun and dynamic when set against colours that fight back. You might not have the courage to use it so boldly, but don't turn your back on it completely. There is no better way to frame a feature, such as this *trompe l'oeil* rug, than by using black. As with red, a little goes a long way in a room. Even if you do not want it at the heart of your decorating schemes, it is worth experimenting with it to introduce an occasional touch of hardness and dynamism.

White is as important as black because the interaction between the colours is so strong. A creamier shade would soften the black slightly, but if you are going for out-and-out dynamism, use brilliant white.

When planning to introduce such dramatic colours to a room, you need a clean canvas on which to work. This is why the walls are painted white. However, to have white woodwork as well would make a room look too stark and clinical, so think about setting the mood by choosing a strong colour for woodwork – maybe black – on the

Right: What is important here is the way the colours fight for attention – white reacts with black; black with blackcurrant; fuchsia with black and so on. This hot pink *chaise longue* is so vibrant it beats black into submission, so becoming a focal point.

framing bold colours

If you want to use colour boldly and really make an impact, think about creating your canvas first. A large room with high ceilings and tall windows is the perfect starting point for something dramatic. By painting it all cream to begin with, you set the stage for some excitement. Bear in mind that this does not have to mean only wall paint: creating one wall of cream drapes brings in another layer of interest, which ultimately helps lift the whole scheme.

window frames and floor. This will have the effect of accentuating the height and size of the room. The stage is now set for other colours to be introduced: choose hot ones, such as aubergine and fuchsia, that will step into the limelight. Now the fun really begins.

The seductive dark purple of blackcurrant is an excellent choice for use with black because it has a similar tonal value. This means that if you were watching an old black-and-white television that showed a room containing both black and blackcurrant objects, your eye would not be able to differentiate between the two. The inspiration for the room shown here came from illustrator Aubrey Beardsley (1872–98), whose work resurfaced when it had an enormous impact on 1960s fashion and design. Beardsley's dandyish image was responsible for the theatrical look of this scheme. The choice of blackcurrant has the right period feeling – something to consider when choosing colours.

Silver also brings a touch of glamour to a room like this, but it has to be a true silver – the wrong shade would look pigeon grey, while gold would look like dull yellow. Once you start bold, stay bold – any compromise would be a mistake. When using hot colours, stoke up the fire, don't try to put it out. After all, if you can't stand the heat, you shouldn't be using this palette.

Right: Drama and glamour are the key words and these have been kept to a pitch through colour and accessories. Using photocopies to create a *découpage* effect on furniture works very successfully; this is then complemented by a touch of silver stencilling on key pieces.

Left: The sense of fun and energy continues with the *découpage* lamp stands, which look as though they have been drawn into place. They complement the Edwardian-style dado stencil in the period-feel blackcurrant perfectly.

stencilled floor 'rug'

Agonizing over whether to have floorboards or carpet? Stop worrying and have both!
Follow Laurence's lead and create a beautiful-looking 'rug' with paint.

1 Prepare the floor by filling holes and sanding if it is in poor condition. Mark out a large square or rectangle (ours was about 2x2m) where you want to position your *trompe l'oeil* rug. Paint black emulsion all around it, then paint the interior fuchsia. To create the black border, use a pencil and long ruler to mark out a stripe about 3cm wide and about 6cm from the edge of the fuchsia. Stick low-tack masking tape on either side of the stripe, then paint it black.

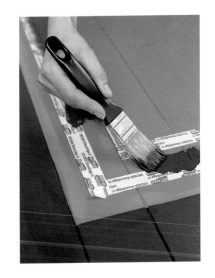

2 Once the paint is dry and the masking tape has been removed, you can draw a freehand design that overlaps the border of the 'rug'. Experiment first on a piece of paper, then draw the design on the floor with a pencil. For interest, we varied the thickness of the lines used in our Art Nouveau-inspired design.

3 Using an artist's paintbrush, fill in the pencil marks with black emulsion. Don't worry if the painted design isn't perfect: it's far enough away from most people's eyes not to matter. Once it's all dry, protect the floor with two coats of acrylic floor varnish.

scarlet
gold and parchment

Red is an uncompromising and energizing choice of colour. In this living room it has been given a twist by being used on wood-work rather than on walls.

Red is energetic, vibrant, bold – the most outrageously extrovert of the Summer Pudding colours – and looks fabulous in Anna Ryder Richardson's oriental living room. Not surprisingly, many people are too scared to use it at all, and viewers of *Changing Rooms* will know that it invariably gets mixed reactions when it is chosen. This is a pity because few other colours make an impact in quite the same way as red. A little goes a very long way, so you can create a wonderfully dramatic effect without ever touching the walls at all. Red is an ideal accessorizing colour and many professional interior decorators think that every room should have a touch of red in it to bring colour schemes together.

Right: Scarlet window frames set the tone for this palatial scheme. Gold wax has been rubbed into the red to give it a slight sheen. This is then echoed by the large gold paisley stamps on the walls.

Red flowers, red picture frames or red rugs are among the most common ways of doing just this, but such small touches are far removed from the in-your-face impact of a red wall.

Red can be teamed with a touch of black and grey for a more architectural feel, or with green – perhaps accented with silver – for a more muted approach. But be warned: red is such an uncompromising colour that whatever you put it with,

the overall effect will be of a red room. If it doesn't stir passion deep within you at first sight, you should probably never go near it at all.

You must begin with some idea of what red will do to a room. For a start, it reduces light, so you need to have enough that this won't matter. Second, it will draw in the walls and ceiling like a cloak. Imagine a room with scarlet walls and cream woodwork – a reverse of the scheme shown here.

painting woodwork

For many years it has been the practice to paint woodwork brilliant white. Happily, this colour rule is now being broken. Using woodwork as the platform for bold gloss colour is a wonderful idea as it is so unexpected and makes dramatic use of the architectural features of a room. You can then bring in another dimension by using coloured wax to rub into the surface so that it catches the light where it is uneven.

Below: The table settings continue the rich oriental theme of this dining room – glasses, candlesticks, plates and cutlery glitter against the wooden table. This was made out of an old door and is supported on plaster elephants.

The intensity of the colour would be far more intimidating. By choosing instead to keep walls neutral and woodwork scarlet, you can achieve the full impact of colour without losing a sense of space.

Skirting boards, picture rails and window frames are often painted off-white to make them invisible in a room, but why not bring them centre stage and make a bold statement instead? White walls would look too stark against the red, but the buttermilk shade used here is warm enough to cope.

All rooms need an accent colour of some sort – a shade that lifts the existing colour even more. Gold is a glorious companion to red as it emphasizes its rich and exotic qualities. Also, if you are going to use bright gloss paint on the woodwork, you can introduce some texture by rubbing it down with a coloured wax. Gold wax on scarlet woodwork gives a sheen as the light hits it.

Right: Dark wood furniture suits the strong colours that surround it – being from the same family, brown, red and gold complement each other well. Oriental-style copper circles have been added to give an authentic touch.

Left: Gold is a wonderful accent colour with red because together they create such a sumptuous effect. Shimmering gold curtains look glamorous and highlight the gold wax rubbed into the woodwork.

Rooms that are out to dazzle can also go over the top when it comes to patterns. In a large, airy room big patterns on the walls emphasize the generous proportions and match the bold character of the colour rather than being submerged by it. If you are lucky enough to have a period house with decorative architectural detailing, such as ornate coving, you can draw attention to it by painting it in the accent colour. This has the effect of emphasizing the height of the room. If, on the other hand, you want to make it less obvious, you could paint the ceiling a slightly darker colour than the walls, which would have the effect of visually lowering it.

Perhaps you like the idea of using such adventurous colour, but would prefer not to end up with too sumptuous a look. If so, consider scaling down the amount of red and gold in the room. Smaller proportions of colour would keep the interest, but take away the force.

Red, cream and gold is a wonderfully warm combination, but it is important to punctuate it with a darker, heavier note so that the effect is not totally overwhelming. Navy blue has weight, so it gives the eye somewhere to pause. Chocolate brown is another possibility, which is why dark wood works so much better than pale with these colours. It has the same tone as the red, so can take the vigour of the crimson.

Red has been ignored for far too long, so it is wonderful to see it back where it belongs – at the heart of decoration. Why not give it a chance to bring some energy into your life?

oriental calligraphy

Anna's attractive and unusual border can be created very simply using tracing paper, pencil and gold paint.

1 First source your oriental lettering – a restaurant or oriental foodstore might be able to help. Draw your lettering on a sheet of A4 paper. Each letter should be about 12cm high. Trace the lettering, using tracing paper, then turn the paper over and retrace. Turn back to the right side and position the paper on the wall using masking tape. Go over the lettering again in pencil.

2 Remove the tracing paper carefully. The pencil lettering should now be transferred to the wall.

3 Use gold paint (we used one by Plastikote) or any other metallic paint to draw over the lettering more emphatically using an artist's brush. Apply two layers of paint if necessary. Don't worry if the lines look slightly wobbly – this can add to the overall character of the room.

wine gums

deep colour

It is a warm autumn day and I am walking down a worn brick path, past the herbaceous borders to the vegetable patch. I am surrounded by the colours of the country and the garden, but they no longer have the definition they had in the summer. These are deep, earthy shades – the ones I like to think of as colours with their edge knocked off.

That bright Chinese yellow found in the Summer Pudding section has taken on the dull gold of olive oil. That brilliant green has faded to sage. The zingy blue to denim. These are very English colours – the faded shades of once-grand country houses. They are also ideal for our northern light because they have a muddiness to them which is very easy on the eye.

Wine Gum shades are not muted – they still have guts – but they are not heart-stoppingly fierce. Think of clothes found in Monsoon or Laura Ashley, with combinations of velvet, chenille, linen and cotton. Think of the fabrics found in flea markets, hand-stitched tapestries, or old-fashioned rose chintzes. This family is comfortable, unassuming and wonderfully easy to use and live with. The colours are nostalgic without being mawkish, and romantic without being at all sentimental.

Out of all the colour families discussed, this one has the most confidence because these colours do not give a hoot about fashion or design. English women have an international reputation for dressing in interesting and rather eccentric ways. (What other nation could have produced both Vivienne Westwood and Alexander McQueen?) Wine Gum colours send out a similar message. They are classic, the most grown-up and show that you, rather than your home, are in charge.

Wine Gums could not be further away from the naturals in their philosophy. Everything and anything goes in these interiors. Granny's old rug? Keep it. A child's cardboard model of a bus? Display it. Dog-eared books? Treasure them. For those who want a cosy life with children, pets and the accumulation of possessions, this palette might well be the one that will suit you.

How to Use Wine Gum Colours

As with Sugared Almonds, these colours work on a simple principle: any colour can go with any other as long as you keep the tone the same. This means that you can mix brick reds with linseed yellows, denims with sages, dusty pinks with pigeon greys. It is not a modern look – far from it in fact – but it has a character that suits a more timeless approach.

Period houses blossom with colours like these; they bring out the charm in rickety sash windows, warped wooden doors and old brick floors. Indeed, they are precisely the sort of colours found in English country houses that have seen better days. The look of faded grandeur is one that we have exported round the world, particularly to the USA and Japan, and these colours are its foundation. They are not so sympathetic to modern spaces because they lack the definition that contemporary architecture requires.

Good light is a boon to all colour schemes, but it is not so essential to Wine Gum colours: their muddiness means that they can cope with the dullest of rooms. This makes them ideal for our changing seasons, too, because their beauty is not lost in the greyness of winter. None the less, you will appreciate them more if you light them well with table lamps and wall lights, as well as overhead bulbs.

Be careful what other colours you introduce. Deep colours are not happy partnered with nat-

urals, pastels or vivids: you must select colours that match their tonal value. This means playing down accent colours, which could put the whole scheme out of balance. Instead, you can introduce contrast through texture – a beautiful damask throw or deep velvet cushion will lift the subtle colours surrounding it. Pattern is permissible, but, like the colours, must not be allowed to dominate. Too much co-ordination would be a mistake, as Wine Gum schemes work best with an unstructured approach. A sofa that goes with a footstool that goes with the curtains would be far too regimented and tailored. In fact, it is the very reason why Americans rarely achieve the English look they so admire, no matter how much money they spend.

The blissful thing about this family of colours is that it is so easy to use. As long as you keep to the idea of tonal value, you can layer a huge number of colours and textures within a room, and it will take on the mellowed charm of a National Trust property.

Ingredients

Plain wooden floorboards topped with faded rugs work best with Wine Gums. Natural floorings, such as sisal and coir, can also look good, but are best used as a base for carpets and rugs.

Traditional hard floors, such as brick, stone or tile, make the perfect foil for the other earthy colours that will be introduced. Fitted carpet, however, will look too smart, and it will be hard to find a shade that blends with the walls.

Windows can be treated very simply or very elaborately; swags and tails would be appropriate, as long as they don't look too new, but so would simple curtains hung from a wooden pole. Fabric, rather than blinds or shutters, comes into its own in Wine Gum schemes. If you love old-fashioned chintzes with full-blown roses, this is the family for you. Scour auction houses, junk shops and

jumble sales for old fabrics you can use or take new ones and soak them in tea for that faded look.

Furniture of dark wood is best. You could try to introduce other materials, such as metal and glass, but they will not be very happy here. It would be rather like presenting an elderly maiden aunt with a Philippe Starck doorknob. Better to browse around your local junk shops and find pieces that can be spruced up a little – not too much because the more distressed they appear, the more at home they will look. The patination that comes with age is a definite plus here.

You need lots of accessories in Wine Gum rooms: big tapestry cushions, numerous photo frames, homely paintings, bowls of pot pourri and flourishing pot plants. It can be a very smart look – think Nina Campbell and the vogue for shabby chic – or it can go in the opposite direction and become very bohemian like an artist's studio-cum-living room. Parents will appreciate rooms like this because children's models made out of cereal packets and play-dough will sit happily

beside more valuable family treasures. Not everything has to be tasteful. The idea is to rise above
all that and do your own thing. That feeling of
anything goes is why these Wine Gum shades
remain such perennial favourites.

The Final Result

Personality is the key word here. Colours like this
are a far cry from fashion catwalks, cutting-edge
magazine covers or the whims of design gurus.
They have little to do with what is happening in
New York, Paris or Milan. The success of a Wine
Gums scheme does not rely on a confident use of
colour or an original use of texture. It is about
what you yourself bring to a room: the things you
own, the way you live, the imprint you make on
your surroundings. It is everything to do with
comfort, cosiness and character. Of the four colour
sections in this book, this is the one I can guarantee will still be around in a decade's time.

Certainly there is a traditional feel to these
colours, and a rural one. The vivids are so much
more urban and architectural; the pastels so modern; the neutrals so global. These colours have their
roots in the earth and to love them you have to be
sympathetic to that aspect of them. They are also
an excellent choice for anyone who hates
decorating and wants to do it as rarely as possible.
In fact, you need never decorate again with these
colours. Instead, you can just keep adding to your
home over the years.

Shaker green and sharp
yellow make a delightful
combination in this
spacious kitchen. The wall
units have been painted
cream to keep the airy feel
of the room.

sage, lemon
and clotted cream

The strong sage green I have used in this kitchen is reminiscent
of Shaker style. It is fresh, clean and confident – ideal for a tired
space where you want to inject new life. It is also very easy to
live with and won't make you gasp for breath when it goes on
the wall. Kitchens and bathrooms are notoriously expensive to
revamp, but the joy of using a colour like this is that a few cans
of paint really can make all the difference to the whole ambience
of a room. This comfortable quality is what sets the Wine Gums
palette apart from the Summer Pudding one.

Left: White can be a surprisingly intrusive colour, so this cumbersome fridge-freezer was painted green to match the units. It has the effect of drawing the eye to the adjacent glass-fronted kitchen cabinet.

Opposite: The mood here is homely and comfortable – a simple wooden table and gingham runner enhance the effect. Even in the town, fresh flowers add a country touch.

A green like this is pleasant to live with because it contains lots of red, which stops it from appearing acidic. Since it has no sharpness, it combines well with other shades, particularly those of the same tone. And using cream for wall units rather than white brings out the muddy warmth of the sage: white would look too stark. Kitchens are always a problem because you do not want to decorate them very often and disrupt the running of your home. It is, therefore, best to choose shades – such as this sage green – that are classic enough to look good for a number of years and that you will not tire of too quickly.

This green is the sort of shade that lends itself very well to solid colour, or to paint effects such as dragging and sponging. The combination of the

unifying space

If you have a room that was originally two or three separate rooms, chances are you have architectural features, such as rolled steel joists, separating each area. However, the new space can be unified with colour, so choose a shade that can be used in large quantities. You can also explore ways of making heavy structural joists less visible. Linda used a stencil on the one here, which softened its appearance.

two – flat colour and textured colour – is ideal for a room where you might have tarted-up junk-shop pieces as well as items made from new timber. The former will probably need layers of flat colour to

disguise their original state, while the latter might look significantly better with the grain of the wood showing through.

However, blocks of flat colour are where decorating fashion is taking us next. This style is a way of drawing attention towards the intensity of particular colours rather than breaking them up though paint techniques. But this does not mean

Right: A plate of real lemons is the inspiration for the motif of the stencil, which has also been painted on to a fabric roller blind (see project overleaf).

Left and above: Stencils can look old-fashioned if you don't make them bold enough, so always go a notch braver than you previously intended. The interesting thing in this kitchen is how well the design lends itself to different materials.

Left: Warm and sympathetic paint shades can make all the difference to drab existing kitchen units. The homely feeling is emphasised with simple and natural accessories such as wicker baskets, creamy earthenware and a wooden worktop.

that you have to use blocks of the same colour. In a kitchen, for example, it can work very well to draw an imaginary line between the lower half of the room and the upper half. This allows the base units to be painted a stronger colour, which anchors them to the floor, while wall units can be given a lighter look to prevent the scheme from being too heavy. Warm cream is an ideal choice, as it makes the perfect foil for this shade of green. If you do introduce a two-tone colour scheme, it is a good idea to have some sort of boundary separating the two, such as this line of tiles in forest green. However, you should continue this approach right through the room where possible. Brilliant white is not appropriate with colours like this – it looks far too intrusive – so the fridge-freezer also had to be painted. As it would have looked ridiculous to continue the two-tone theme on this, green was chosen to allow it to blend into the room.

Accent colours are vital to accessorize a room.

They have the same effect that scarves, bags and shoes create with a favourite outfit. Lemon yellow is perfect for a green and cream scheme, as it has a sharpness that lifts both colours, but other possible accents could be tomato red, or even a touch of black if a more dramatic look is required.

Remember to consider scale when designing a room. Stencils are still an excellent way of bringing visual interest to the walls, and the larger the scale, the better. Now that decoration is used with so much more confidence, stencilling something small and fiddly looks dated. Go for impact by making them as big as possible, particularly in a room where you have a strong base colour such as sage green.

Naturals match both these key shades very well without distracting attention from the main colour story. Unpainted bricks and earthy floor tiles blend very well into Wine Gum schemes. They act as a foil for the more definite shades, but prevent the whole scheme becoming overwhelming.

stencilled blind

The stencil of lemons and leaves adds a bold, fresh look to this kitchen. It's also as easy to apply to the fabric blind as it is to the walls.

1 Draw or trace your stencil design on to a piece of stencil card, using any image you like: it might be from a magazine, book or any copyright-free source. Shade the parts of the design that will be cut away. Remember to leave solid parts within the design so that your stencil will not fall apart.

2 Cut out the shaded parts using a sharp craft knife on a suitable cutting surface, such as old vinyl offcuts – you don't want to ruin your table-top.

3 Use a little spray mount adhesive or tape to hold the stencil in place on the blind. Using a stencil brush, apply water-based acrylic paint through the stencil. Go for a soft, cloudy look.

This child's room is suitably invigorating and stimulating – primary colours have been slightly toned down to Wine Gum shades to provide a colour scheme that is rich in inspiration.

mustard, flax
and burnt orange

Wine Gum colours are a couple of steps away from the no-holds-barred intensity of the vivids. But, because they are a notch down, that doesn't mean they can't be bold. Mustard, flax and burnt orange are more sophisticated and enlivening than the classic primary colours – blue, yellow and red – so often used in children's bedrooms, playdens, family rooms and kitchens. Here Michael Jewitt has designed a dramatic and visually exciting playroom with lots of child appeal.

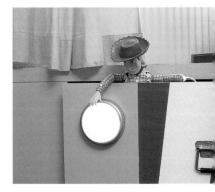

Paddington & Co. 1999

Above and above right:
The theme for the room
is of a construction site,
so accessories have been
chosen that complement
this. Curtains are made of
clear PVC to mock up a
lorry windscreen.

Right: One of the reasons
the room works so well is
that there is something
happening whichever way
you look – these stencilled
logos add another
dimension to the strong
Wine Gum colour scheme.

Disney characters © Disney Enterprises, Inc. Used by permission from Disney Enterprises, Inc.

Bold colours are usually associated with children rather than adults, but there are plenty of ideas that can be plundered for grown-up schemes. The colours here all work well together, but rather than focusing the eye on the walls, it might be better to disperse them throughout a room and use only a couple of shades. Mustard walls combined with blue furniture create a Provençal feeling, whereas blue walls with orange detailing create a more modern look.

If you do want to use them all together, it might be better to keep walls to one or two shades and use the others for flooring, furniture and accessories. Introduce a touch of black to give them an edge.

A scheme like this relies more than any other on the idea of tonal value. This means that you can line up a whole series of colours, all of them unrelated at first glance, but none will jump out at you or dominate the group because they all share the same tone. One of the difficulties of choosing colours from paint charts is that you flick backwards and forwards trying to assess whether certain colours work together. In fact, you can only really establish this when you see them all in front of you in the finished room. You have to learn to rely on

Left: The building site theme continues with rubber tyres on the walls. These are visually bold and strong enough to sustain the weight of a child – safety is paramount in a room such as this.

Above: Attention to detail makes all the difference to the success of a scheme – using spanners as handles is an inspired choice which adds wit to the scheme.

Right: This climbing wall had to be checked and double-checked for safety before allowing a child on it, but it proved a huge hit.

Care Bears™ © Those Characters From Cleveland, Inc.

your instincts. Successfully combining colours can be learnt only through trial and error.

Colours do affect mood, of course, and these shades are all stimulating, so it is quite brave to use them in a child's bedroom. Will he or she ever sleep? However, when the bedroom doubles as a playroom, it makes perfect sense. Designs like the one illustrated here will keep the mind active and

the imagination fertile. Huge blocks of colour on the walls can be the first step towards creating a fantasy world. Explore the possibility of making drama out of colour alone, rather than using applied decoration to break it down, or adding texture to soften it. You want to create a buzz the moment the door is opened.

Each colour should be placed next to another

Disney characters © Disney Enterprises, Inc. Used by permission from Disney Enterprises, Inc. Garfield © PAWS.

Left: Once you begin with an idea, it is likely to fire the imagination and take over. Even favourite toys are catered for with these chevron-decorated sleeping bags that can be hung up ready for bedtime.

to give maximum impact: yellow with blue, for instance. The fabulous thing about such a theatrical use of colour is that it really does have an uplifting effect. Everyone who walks in will love it because it has such a feel-good factor. If you do have a space in your home where you want to feel stimulated rather than calm and relaxed, you should

which colour?

Choosing paint colours is very difficult because it is so hard to visualize what one tiny square of paint will look like when applied to a large expanse of wall. If you don't have time to mess about with sample pots, find the colour you really love, but order the shade that appears to be a couple of notches down from it. You will probably find that, once painted, it looks exactly like the colour you first so admired.

think about using colour to achieve the right atmosphere. A kitchen would be an excellent place to start, as would a family room or play den. Expect to see a lot more intense colour like this in the future: soon it won't be just children having all the fun.

If you want to achieve maximum visual stimulation, make sure that no colour is left alone – there could be something on every wall to capture the attention. It might be a graphic logo, such as a warning triangle, or perhaps yellow and black zigzags, which could become the frame for other features. Take some risks, too. Silver is not an obvious accent colour with the Wine Gums palette, but the current trend is to introduce small amounts of metallics wherever possible. Scarlet is a more obvious accent shade, but by using it in small portions, it is not allowed to dominate.

The wonderful thing about decorating children's rooms is that you can be as bold as you want. Kids love over-the-top schemes full of colour and character, so you can open those paint cans and really enjoy yourself. There are simply no boundaries.

stencilled warning sign

Once again, masking tape is the key to success in copying Michael's realistic-looking wall symbols. You can make your own stencils to customize them in any way you like.

Disney characters © Disney Enterprises, Inc. Used by permission from Disney Enterprises, Inc. Garfield © PAWS.

1 Once the base coat is dry, mask out a triangle on the wall. This one is equi-lateral, but I have rounded the edges by eye. Mask off the curves by using small amounts of low-tack masking tape. Apply the blue colour, using two coats if necessary.

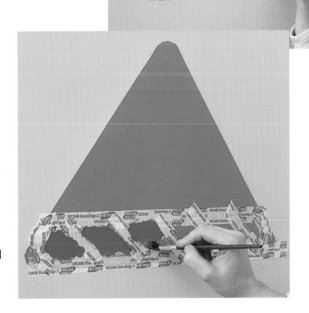

2 Once the blue has dried, create the striped pattern by masking off diagonal stripes along the base. Use red emulsion or acrylic paint and apply with an artist's brush. Once this is dry, remove the centre pieces of tape. Apply new pieces of tape to protect the edges of the red and fill in the rest of the striped band with white paint.

3 Design and cut out your own lettering stencil, using a ruler to ensure the letter sides are even. Remember to leave bridges so that parts of the design don't fall apart. Hold it in place on the wall with some spray adhesive or masking tape. Apply the yellow lettering paint with a stencil brush.

honey,
orange
and bitter chocolate

This African-inspired scheme uses rich honey, dark brown and warm neutrals to bring back memories of exotic travels and create a nostalgic, colonial-style living space.

Rich, warm and inviting, honey brings character to any room. This makes it one of the most important and versatile of the Wine Gums shades. However, with such a dense colour, there is always a danger that it will make a room appear smaller, so it is best used in a room with fairly generous proportions and good light. Luckily this living room is huge. The trick is to use some sort of applied decoration that will give the illusion of looking through to the solid colour behind. Colour-washing achieves this, as do stencilling, dragging, sponging and many other paint effects. The introduction of a second strong colour adds guts to a mid-tone colour that might otherwise appear too cloying.

choosing furniture

Above: The room is not overlooked, which meant that there was no need to spend money on window treatments. Instead a feature was made of this area with a built-in seat and plenty of comfortable scatter cushions.

Above: The look here is unfussy – this simple bamboo mat is lashed together with string. The idea was to create a scheme that looked thrown together with ease.

If you choose a strong wall colour, you will have to make sure that your furniture is bold enough to take it. Pale furniture should be stained dark brown in a room with a very forceful colour personality. Furniture legs provide another way of breaking up colour and allowing the eye to look through to the walls beyond. You can go really over the top with this idea, like the multi-legged window seat shown here. The legs add a sort of sculptural quality to the room, creating another layer of interest.

Remember that it is possible to change the mood of a colour entirely. Chocolate brown and honey are natural companions, but black could be used instead of brown for a more dramatic effect – perfect for a dining room used mainly at night. One of the attractions of honey is that it looks beautiful in all kinds of artificial light. It has a seductive quality that makes it ideal for rooms that are used mainly in the evening.

The earthy combination of yellow and brown has strong associations with Africa, so you might choose to create a naive art look with wobbly lines and irregular block-printing. However, it is possible to create quite a different result by combining ochre with jewel-like greens, blues and metallic gold for a rich, palatial feeling, or to give it a honeyed softness with soothing creams and whites. Honey really does have a surprising range

Above and below: A basic block-printed design and freehand stripes were used to accentuate the naive feel. Imperfections add character and should be left alone.

of possibilities. The core colour is only the starting point, not the end of the story.

Having chosen the wall colour, you should now think about which complementaries to bring in. Golds and browns are natural companions to honey, and by keeping the wall and floor roughly the same shade, you can unify the scheme and create a golden canvas on which to work. This shade of yellow is so strong that dark brown furniture will work much better than pale woods. It is also the sort of colour that can take quite heavy, chunky shapes. In fact, it demands a bold approach: go too gently and you will feel submerged by it. And don't assume that a room will inevitably look

Left: Offcuts from old railway sleepers were used to make rough-edged display shelves; they make the perfect setting for treasures brought back from Africa, such as these carved heads.

Left: The coffee table is made from an old concrete paving slab and recycled legs. The *papier-maché* container was specially made to hold popcorn – such personal touches make a room.

smaller once the furniture is in place: this is not necessarily so. If the colour has been broken up in one of the ways suggested earlier, the walls will appear to recede as you look through the top colour to the one behind it. That is why breaking up colour is so important. All colours play visual tricks like this, so don't panic when first putting up paint. You really can't get an idea of the overall effect until the whole scheme is complete.

Rooms tend to look boring if there is no excitement and risk, so now break the rules by introducing a shade that demands attention. Tangy orange adds zing – a hint of sharpness that punctuates the yellow and stops it from being too cloying and sickly. Acid green or cherry red would make a similarly powerful statement, but the orange works particularly well because it comes

from the same earthy family as the honey and brown. Accent colours are vital in a room where one colour is very dominant; they lift the entire scheme and bring all the elements together.

This is why accessorizing is tremendously important in any room. Colour is not just about walls – it is also about all the small touches that make up a scheme. In a room where you have chosen colours from the same family, you could introduce natural shades that have textural interest, such as stone, wheat or wood. They will add visual interest without fighting with the dominant colours. Honey is one of the most satisfying shades to work with: it floods a room with colour, yet does so without aggression. And because it is so versatile, you can play around with it until you find the best way of making it work for you.

Left: The fireplace was made from an old railway sleeper, which is in keeping with the artisan style of the room. A row of Newcastle Brown beer bottles indicates the home city and matches the colour scheme perfectly.

freehand stripes and blocking

Geometrical precision is not always a good idea where pattern is concerned.
In this warm-looking ochre living room stripes were painted freehand to give a more
relaxed feeling. The diamond-pattern dado 'rail' is stamped using two differently
shaped triangular sponges.

1 Once the base coat on the walls is dry, begin painting the vertical lines down from the dado. Start work on one section of wall and put in the centre line first. After this, add the quarters, and between these build up your pattern of stripes, always working from the centre outwards. A wobbly line and uneven application of paint are fine here. Use a thinned emulsion (2:1 paint to water) to get a fluid line.

2 Once all the lines in the room are dried, make the first half of your stamp to create the dado 'rail'. Cut a decorator's sponge into a triangle. Tip a little of the emulsion colour on to a plate and thin the paint 2:1 as before. Dip just the face of the sponge into the paint, then press on to the edge of the dado line at regular intervals.

3 Make the second half of the stamp pattern by cutting a sponge into a V-shape. Use the same technique as before to apply the paint to the dado.

stockists and suppliers

Paints

ARTHUR SANDERSON & SONS (Information line: 01895 238 244)

CROWN PAINTS, Akzo Nobel Decorative Coatings Ltd, PO Box 37, Crown House, Hollins Road, Darwen, Lancs BB3 0BG. (01254) 704951

DULUX PAINTS, The Dulux Advice Centre, ICI Paints, Wexham Road, Slough, Berks SL2 5DS. (01753) 550555

JOHNSTONES PAINTS (Decorator Centre), Unit 3, 401–405 Oldfield Lane North, Greenford, Middx UB6 8QE. (0181 575 1604

LIVING ROOMS, 172 Leith Walk, Edinburgh EH6 5EB. (0131) 561 1903

PAPERS AND PAINTS, 4 Park Walk, London SW10 0AD. (0171) 352 8626 (Also available by mail order)

DIY Materials

B & Q (Information line: 0181 466 4166)

DO IT ALL (Information line: 0800 436436)

GREAT MILLS RETAIL LTD, RMC House, Paulton, Bristol BS39 7SX. (01761) 416034

RAY MUNN, 861–863 Fulham Road, London. (0171) 736 9876

Furnishings and Fabrics

HABITAT (Store information line: 0645 334433 – local rate calls)

HOMEBASE LTD, Beddington House, Railway Approach, Wallington, Surrey SM6 0HB. (0181) 784 7200

JOHN LEWIS PARTNERSHIP, 278/306 Oxford Street, London W1A 1EX. (0171) 629 7711

THE NATURAL FABRIC COMPANY, Wessex Place, 127 High Street, Hungerford, Berks RG17 0DL. (01488) 684002 (Shop and mail order)

THE PIER, 91/95 King's Road, London SW3 4PA. (Enquiry line: 0171 814 5020)

SELFRIDGES, 400 Oxford Street, London W1A 1AB. (0171) 629 1234

Specialist suppliers

THE MOSAIC WORKSHOP, 443–449 Holloway Road, London N7 6LJ. (0171) 263 2997. (Mail order service and courses)

PLASTERWORKS, 38 Cross Street, London N1 2BG. (0171) 226 5355 (For statuary and plaster decorations, e.g. ceiling roses)

THE STENCIL STORE GROUP PLC, 20/21 Heronsgate Road, Chorleywood, Herts WD3 5BN. (01923) 285577 (Store information, mail order and workshops)

paint listings

Below is a room-by-room listing of the paints used in the featured rooms:

Café au lait and mocha
Walls: Stucco – Full Fat Cream, Ray Munn.
Matt emulsion – Get Stoned, Ray Munn (below dado).

Sea-grey, cobalt and sand
Walls and ceiling: Vinyl matt emulsion – aqua blue E12-41, aqua green E11-21, dove grey OO A 05, Leyland Paints.
Matt emulsion – brilliant white, Wickes.

Ivory, aubergine and white
Walls and ceiling: Cotton twill dustsheet (12ft x 12ft), Stanley.

Ice blue, denim and silver
Walls: Leyland matt emulsion – nippy Q20.
Leyland matt emulsion – apple cross R37.
Odds'n'ends chrome spray-paint, Plasti-Kote.
B & Q vinyl matt emulsion – brilliant white.

Camomile, sage and coral
Walls: Sanderson YTaupe Brown W-513M.
Sanderson Orange Bloom Lt–5020P. White paint washed over base paints.

Lilac, blueberry and silver
Walls and woodwork; Vinyl matt emulsion – zinnia 030 (lilac), marlborough N7 (darker lilac), ice mountain N1 (pale lavender), Leyland Paints.
Quick-drying eggshell – ice mountain N1 (pale lavender), Leyland Paints.
Ceiling: Vinyl matt emulsion – zinnia 030 (lilac), ice mountain N1 (pale lavender), Leyland Paints.

Fuchsia and blackcurrant
Walls: Dulux Once emulsion – ivory lace.
Dulux Once Emulsion – brilliant white.
Dulux Gloss – 30RB09/179 (aubergine).
Floor: Crown vinyl silk black emulsion.
Dulux vinyl matt emulsion – 01RR16/397.
Aqualac matt floor varnish, Foxell and James.
General-purpose clear gloss floor varnish, Ronseal.

Tutti-frutti ice-cream
Walls and woodwork: One-coat white emulsion, Wickes.
Dulux vinyl matt emulsion match pots.

Scarlet, gold and parchment
Walls: Dulux silk emulsion – 25YY80/187.
Dulux metallic paint – burnished gold.
Woodwork and skirting: Dulux vinyl matt emulsion – 30YR13/471.
Gold treasure wax, The Reeves Shop.
Ceiling rose and covering: Antique-gold metallic spray-paint, Plasti-Kote.

Sage, lemon and clotted cream
Units: ESP (Easy Surface Preparation), Ray Munn.
Dulux quick-drying satinwood – 30GY34/249 (green), 30YY80/106 (cream).
Stencilling: Artists' acrylic paints, London Graphic Centre.
Walls: Dulux vinyl matt emulsion – 30YY80/106 (cream).
Dulux quick-drying satinwood – 30GY34/249 (green).

Honey, orange and bitter chocolate
Walls: Johnstone vinyl matt emulsion E5-28 (yellow ochre), E5-19 (mushroom), E5-20 (dark brown).

Mustard, flax and burnt orange
Walls: Vinyl matt emulsion/eggshell – glory days B14 (yellow), Columbus R31 (blue), Leyland Paints.
Vinyl matt emulsion – 68YR 34/780 (orange), Dulux.
Quick-drying Satinwood – 68R 34/780 (orange), Dulux.

Picture Credits

BBC Books would like to thank the following for providing photographs and for permission to reproduce copyright material. While every effort has been made to trace and acknowledge all copyright holders, we would like to apologize should there have been any errors or omissions.

All photographs by Ed Reeve © BBC 1999 Worldwide, except the following:

BBC Good Homes Magazine 9r, 22b, 54t, 81, 82, 84b Ed Reeve, 13b Tim Young, 15t, 21, 51m, 52, Steve Dalton, 15b Marie Louise Avery, 19 Neil Mersh, 20t Nadia McKenzie, 22 PSC, 23t, 112 Niall Mcdiarmid, 12,116 Robin Matthews 23b, 50b Hannah Lewis, 55 Tom Leighton, 83b Tim Imrie, 84t Polly Wreford, 85 Lucinda Symons.

BBC Homes & Antiques 113m, 114/115, 117b.

BBC Worldwide 20b Philip Webb, 83t Nick Carman.

Robert Harding Picture Library 10 Ray Rainford; Images Colour Library 8t, 10/11, 51, 54b, 80, 115; Telegraph Colour Library 8b, 18, 50t, 113, 117t.

index